CAMBRIDGE
UNIVERSITY PRESS

Click Start

INTERNATIONAL EDITION

Learner's Book 4

CAMBRIDGE
UNIVERSITY PRESS

Shaftesbury Road, Cambridge CB2 8EA, United Kingdom

One Liberty Plaza, 20th Floor, New York, NY 10006, USA

477 Williamstown Road, Port Melbourne, VIC 3207, Australia

314–321, 3rd Floor, Plot 3, Splendor Forum, Jasola District Centre, New Delhi – 110025, India

103 Penang Road, #05–06/07, Visioncrest Commercial, Singapore 238467

Cambridge University Press is part of the University of Cambridge.

It furthers the University's mission by disseminating knowledge in the pursuit of education, learning and research at the highest international levels of excellence.

www.cambridge.org
Information on this title: www.cambridge.org/9781108951869

© Cambridge University Press & Assessment 2021

First published 2021

20 19 18 17 16 15 14 13 12 11 10 9 8 7 6

Printed in the Netherlands by Wilco BV

ISBN 978-1-108-95186-9 Paperback

Cambridge University Press has no responsibility for the persistence or accuracy of URLs for external or third-party internet websites referred to in this publication, and does not guarantee that any content on such websites is, or will remain, accurate or appropriate. Information regarding prices, travel timetables, and other factual information given in this work is correct at the time of first printing but Cambridge University Press does not guarantee the accuracy of such information thereafter.

....

....

Every effort has been made to trace the owners of copyright material included in this book. The publishers would be grateful for any omissions brought to their notice for acknowledgement in future editions of the book.

Introduction

The international edition of **Click Start: Computing for Schools** is designed around the latest developments in the field of computer science, information and communication technology. Based on Windows 7 and MS Office 2010, with extensive updates on Windows 10 and MS Office 2016, the series aids the understanding of the essentials of computer science including computer basics, office applications, creative software, programming concepts and programming languages.

Each level of the series has been designed keeping in mind the learning ability of the learners as well as their interests. Efforts have been made to use examples from day-to-day life, which will help the learners to bridge the gap between their knowledge of the subject and the real world. The books are designed to offer a holistic approach and help in the overall development of the learners.

KEY FEATURES

- **Snap Recap:** Probing questions to begin a chapter and assess pre-knowledge
- **Learning Objectives:** A list of the learning outcomes of the chapter
- **Activity:** Interactive exercise after every major topic to reinforce analytical skills and application-based learning
- **Exercise:** A variety of questions to test understanding
- **Fact File:** Interesting concept-related facts to improve concept knowledge
- **Quick Key** and **Try This:** Shortcuts and useful tips on options available for different operations
- **Glossary:** Chapter-end list of important terms along with their definitions
- **You Are Here:** Quick recap
- **Lab Work:** Practical exercises to enable application of concepts through learning-by-doing
- **Project Work:** Situational tasks to test practical application of the concepts learnt
- **Who Am I?:** Biographies to inspire young learners
- **Sample Paper:** Practice and preparation for exams

The aim of this book is to make learning fun and to help the learners achieve a certain level of expertise in this fast-changing world of computer science.

Overview

Snap Recap
Probing questions to begin a chapter and assess pre-knowledge

SNAP RECAP
1. What is a computer?
2. Explain the terms – input, process and output.
3. What is computer hardware?
4. What is software? Discuss the various types of software.
5. Using suitable examples, differentiate between computer hardware and software.
6. What is an operating system?

Learning Objectives
A list of the learning outcomes of the chapter

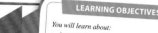
LEARNING OBJECTIVES
You will learn about:
- input devices – keyboard, mouse, joystick, light pen, touch screen, scanner, barcode reader, digital camera and web camera
- output devices – monitor, printer, plotter and speakers
- central processing unit
- primary and secondary memory
- specific applications of computers
- limitations of computers

Activity
Interactive exercises after every major topic to reinforce analytical skills and application-based learning

ACTIVITY
Find out about the different types of printers installed in your school and write a few points about each. Take the help of your teacher or use the Internet.

Exercise
A variety of questions to test understanding

EXERCISE
A. Fill in the blanks.
1. .... is the image that you see when the computer is left idle for some time.
2. .... is a collection of related information.
3. The window which is open but is not in use is called ....
4. Windows have a manager called ....
5. In order to set Screen Saver, you need to open .... window.
6. .... is a basic text editor program in Windows.

FACT FILE
You can also access the Personalization window by taking the following path:
Start ⟹ Control Panel ⟹ Personalization option.

Fact File
Interesting concept-related facts to improve concept knowledge

TRY THIS
Select the folder to be deleted. Press the **Delete** key on your keyboard. Click **Yes** in the **Delete Folder** dialog box to confirm deletion.

QUICK KEY
To remove a file/folder permanently without sending it to the Recycle Bin. **Shift + Delete**

Quick Key and Try This
Shortcuts and useful tips on options available for different operations

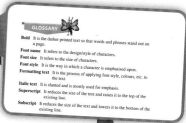

Glossary
Chapter-end list of important terms along with their definitions

GLOSSARY

Bold It is the darker printed text so that words and phrases stand out on a page.
Font name It refers to the design/style of characters.
Font size It refers to the size of characters.
Font style It is the way in which a character is emphasised upon.
Formatting text It is the process of applying font style, colours, etc. to the text.
Italic text It is slanted and is mostly used for emphasis.
Superscript It reduces the size of the text and raises it to the top of the existing line.
Subscript It reduces the size of the text and lowers it to the bottom of the existing line.

You Are Here
Quick recap

YOU ARE HERE 4
1. Stamps can be put on pictures created in Tux Paint.
2. Stamps can be resized and reoriented depending on the requirement.
3. Different types of drawing canvasses are available to use in Tux Paint. A canvas may have a coloured background, black-and-white drawing or a 3-D photograph.
4. A slide show can also be set-up in Tux Paint. The sequence of slides and the speed of slide change can also be specified.
5. The pictures created in Tux Paint can be printed using the Print tool.
6. Label tool is used to write on any object/stamp.

Lab Work
Practical exercises to enable application of concepts through learning-by-doing

LAB WORK

A. In the school lab, find out the different input and output devices available. Make a list of these in MS Word. Put a picture along with one use of each listed input and output devices.
B. Storage devices are used to store our data for future use. Take the help of the Internet and make a list of at least five latest storage devices available in the market these days. Also, write a few lines about each.

PROJECT WORK

Write the MSWLogo commands to assign marks of 5 subjects of a student using five different variables. Find and print the total marks out of 500. Also, calculate the percentage.

Project Work
Situational tasks to test practical application of the concepts learnt

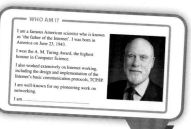

WHO AM I?

I am a famous American scientist who is known as 'the father of the Internet'. I was born in America on June 23, 1943.

I won the A. M. Turing Award, the highest honour in Computer Science.

I also worked extensively on Internet working, including the design and implementation of the Internet's basic communication protocols, TCP/IP.

I am well-known for my pioneering work on networking.

I am ....

Sample Paper
Practice and preparation for exams

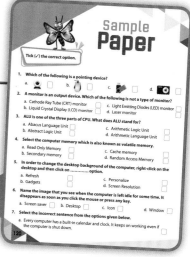

Who Am I?
Biographies to inspire young learners

Contents

Know Your Computer

1

Introduction

You use different parts of a computer to get information. The words you read on the computer screen are written using the signals from the keys you press on the keyboard. The file you save or open is on the hard disk. Different parts of a computer are used to obtain different types of information.

You will now learn more about the basic parts of a computer and their functions.

Input devices

The devices that give data or instructions to the computer are called **input devices**. The most commonly used input devices are the keyboard and mouse.

Keyboard

The keyboard is a commonly used input device. It allows the user to input letters, numbers and other characters into a computer.
It operates like a typewriter, but has many additional keys. It can do many things that a typewriter cannot.

Keyboard

Mouse

As you move the mouse on a mouse pad, a small arrow moves on the screen. The arrow you see on the screen is the pointer. The mouse is also known as a **pointing device**. The pointer follows the movement of the mouse.

The pointer follows the movement of the mouse

There are various types of computer mice. Here you will learn about two basic types of computer mice.

Mouse with a roller ball: A roller ball allows the mouse to move on a flat surface.

Optical mouse: Optical mice are much more commonly used now. They use a light source to detect the movement of the mouse. This in turn allows movement of the pointer on the screen.

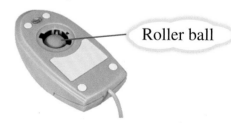

Mouse with a roller ball

Optical mouse

Joystick

Joystick

A joystick is a vertical handle which can be moved forwards, backwards and sideways to control a machine. It is a pointing device that works like a computer mouse as it is used to move the pointer on the computer screen. It is often used for playing computer games.

Touch screen

A **touch screen** is a computer screen that acts both as an input and output device. It is sensitive to the touch of a finger or stylus. We interact with the computer by touching text or pictures displayed on the screen. This is another way of giving input to the computer. Based on the selection made on the screen, you will get the output. A good example is an ATM screen. You can touch different options to help you take money out of the bank. Many laptops are now available with touch screens to make our work easy.

Touch screen

Scanner

A scanner is a device that transfers data – such as hand-drawn pictures or text, photographic prints, posters and magazine pages – into the computer. This is done by converting the input document image into a digital format which can then be fed into the computer.

Scanner

The scanned data can be edited or modified in the computer.

Barcode reader

A barcode is a set of lines of different thicknesses that represent a number. Most packaged products in shops have barcodes on them.

A barcode reader is used to read the barcode given on a package and feed the information into the computer. The number is then used by the computer for preparing the bill with relevant details of the item including name, quantity and price.

Barcode reader

Digital camera

A digital camera records images in a digital form which can be stored in a computer. These images in the camera can also be printed.

Digital cameras are also used for video recording.

Digital camera

Web camera

A web camera records moving pictures and sound, and allows these to be broadcasted on the internet as they happen. It is used mainly for video chatting and video conferencing.

Web camera

Output devices

The devices that display a result or information are called **output devices**. This information is displayed on the monitor. It can also be printed on paper using a printer.

Monitor

A monitor is also known as a **Visual Display Unit** (VDU). It is an output device that looks like a television. It displays both text and pictures. The output that is displayed on the monitor is called the **soft copy**. There are three main types of monitors available for computers.

Cathode Ray Tube (CRT) monitors: CRT monitors are the oldest type of monitor that look like an old bulky television set. They are heavy in size and less expensive.

CRT monitor

Liquid Crystal Display (LCD) monitors: LCD monitors have replaced CRT monitors as they are thinner, lighter and occupy less space. LCD technology is currently used in making screens for televisions, laptops, calculators, etc.

The only disadvantage is that the picture loses its clarity when we try viewing the screen from different angles.

Light Emitting Diodes (LED) monitors: This is a better technology than CRT and LCD and is now used everywhere. They consume less electricity as compared to CRT and LCD monitors. The screen displays images very clearly.

Flat screen monitor

Since LED and LCD monitors come in a flat screen display, they are also known as **flat screen monitors**.

Printer

A printer gives the output on paper. It prints exactly what is seen on the screen. The printout from the printer is called the **hard copy**.

Based on the technology used, printers can be classified as **impact** or **non-impact printers**.

Hard Copy

Impact printer: This uses the typewriting printing mechanism where there is a direct contact between the paper and the print head, for example, dot-matrix and character printers.

Dot-matrix printer: It has a matrix of small pins that are moved around on the page to form a pattern of dots depending on the type of image or text to be printed. These are not commonly used anymore, but have limited special purposes in some businesses.

Dot-matrix printer

Non-impact printer: This does not touch the paper while printing. It uses chemical, heat or electrical signals to print the symbols on paper. For example, inkjet, deskjet, laser and thermal printers. These are the most common types of printer used at home and in offices.

Inkjet printer: This usually prints in color by spraying out small dots of ink onto the paper. It works faster than the dot-matrix printer and produces better quality images.

Inkjet printer

Laser printer

Laser printer: This uses a laser beam to print on paper. This type of printer is very fast and images are high quality.

Plotter

This is a device that draws pictures on paper, based on the commands received from a computer. Plotters differ from other printers as they draw lines using a pen. They can produce continuous lines, where other printers can only print lines as a closely spaced series of dots. Large printouts of drawings can be made on paper using plotters.

Plotter

Speakers

Speakers generate sound, based on the input given, which the listener can hear. Speakers of specific range are built in to all computers and laptops.

If the sound is required to be audible to a large group of listeners, then speakers of higher frequency can be attached as an output device to the computer.

Speakers

ACTIVITY

Find out about the different types of printers installed in your school and write a few points about each. Ask your teacher for help or use the internet.

Central Processing Unit

Once information is sent to a computer by one of the input devices, it is processed. The **Central Processing Unit** (CPU) is the brain of the computer. It processes the information.

The CPU is divided into three parts:

1. **ALU** stands for **Arithmetic Logic Unit**. It carries out all mathematical and logical calculations.

2. **CU** stands for **Control Unit**. It controls the flow of information in the system. It works like a traffic policeman who controls the traffic on the road.

3. **MU** stands for **Memory Unit**. It holds the processed and unprocessed data. Memory is a container that holds the data of a computer.

Computer memory

A computer has a huge storage capacity. The storage capacity of a computer is called its **memory**. It enables the computer to store data and instructions. As you measure distance in kilometres, time in seconds, weight in kilograms, the memory is measured in bytes.

FACT FILE

The computer converts data into the smallest unit, known as a bit (**bi**nary digi**t**). The computer understands only two types of bits, 0 and 1. Bits are usually assembled into a group of eight to form a byte.

8 Bits	= 1 Byte	1024 MB	= 1 Gigabyte (GB)
1024 Bytes	= 1 Kilobyte (KB)	1024 GB	= 1 Terabyte (TB)
1024 KB	= 1 Megabyte (MB)		

There are two types of computer memory: **primary memory** and **secondary memory**.

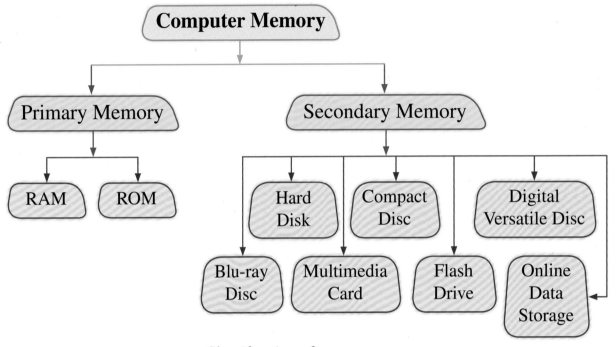

Classification of computer memory

Primary memory

Primary memory is necessary for a computer to work. It is also called the **internal memory**. It is the main area where data is stored. The stored data can be recalled and processed by the CPU. The end result is displayed on the output device. There are two types of primary memory: **RAM** and **ROM**.

RAM

RAM stands for **Random Access Memory**. It holds instructions for the computer, its programs and the data. Information can be read on RAM and written or changed onto it. Hence, it is also known as read/write memory. *However, it is temporary in nature.* Therefore, it is also called **volatile memory**. The stored data disappears when the computer is shut down. That is why you are always advised to save your work.

TRY THIS

To check the primary memory (RAM) of your computer:

Go to the Control Panel ⟹ System and Security ⟹ System

What is its unit and capacity?

ROM

ROM stands for **Read Only Memory**. Information can only be read from it and not written or changed. The information it contains is the **Basic Input–Output System** or BIOS, which is used to load the operating system. ROM is the built-in memory of a computer. The stored data does not disappear even when the computer is shut down. *Therefore, it is permanent in nature*. It is also called **non-volatile memory**.

Secondary memory

When you work on a computer, it stores information temporarily. As soon as it is shut down, the information is lost. So you need a place where you can store data on a long-term basis. This will ensure that data can be used when required.

The memory where the data is stored on a long-term basis is called the secondary memory. The information stored is not lost even when the computer is shut down. It is also known as the **backup memory** or the **external memory**. It is stored in places other than the primary memory of a computer. For example, on hard disks, compact discs (CDs), flash drives, Blu-ray discs, multimedia cards, etc.

Hard disk

A hard disk can store lots of data and provides relatively quick access to that data. The data is stored on an electromagnetically charged surface or set of surfaces. The hard

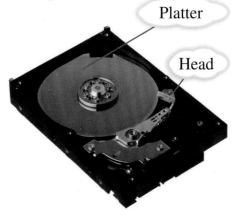

Platter

Head

Structure of a hard disk drive

disk is generally fitted inside the CPU box. Computers are available with a hard disk that has storage capacity in terms of gigabytes (GB) and terabytes (TB).

A hard disk is made up of a collection of discs called **platters**. These are stacked on a cylindrical rod. Each rod has data recorded electromagnetically in concentric circles or **tracks** on the disk. Tracks are further divided into **sectors**.

A head reads or writes the information on the tracks with the help of the Hard Disk Drive (HDD).

A **portable hard disk** (also known as a **portable hard drive**) is a mass storage device designed to be easily transported and externally connected to a computer. Portable HDDs are available that can store up to 2 TB (2 Terabytes = 2048 GB) of data.

Advantages of a hard disk

1. It stores a large amount of data.
2. It is highly reliable as it is less prone to data damage.

Disadvantage of a hard disk

It is quite expensive.

Compact Disc

A Compact Disc (CD) is a portable, round disc used for recording, storing and playing audio, video, text and other information in a digital form. It was originally developed to store sound recordings. Later, it also allowed the preservation of other types of data.

Compact disc

A standard CD has a diameter of 120 mm. It stores up to 80 minutes of uncompressed audio (737 MB of data). A mini CD or pocket CD has a diameter ranging from 60 to 80 mm. These can store up to 24 minutes of audio.

Different types of CD

1. *CD-ROM*: The data can be written once but read any number of times using a CD-ROM drive fixed into the CPU of the computer.

2. *CD-RW*: Can be used for both reading and writing data. The written data can be erased and new data can be written on it multiple times.

3. *CD-R*: It can record data or music only once.

Advantages of a CD

1. It is easy to use.

2. It has high storage capacity.

Disadvantages of a CD

1. It is sensitive to heat and light.

2. It is more prone to data damage.

Digital Versatile Disc

A newer technology, the **Digital Versatile Disc** (DVD), stores a minimum of 4.7 GB of data and is used for playing movies. A DVD drive is needed to use the DVD.

DVD

Blu-ray Disc

Like CD and DVD, a Blu-ray disc is also a circular disc that is used as a storage device. It is used for recording and playing video in high-definition (HD). It can store up to 25 GB of data due to the blue-violet laser technology it uses. It requires a Blu-ray reader to be fitted into the computer where it is being used.

Blu-ray disk

Multimedia card

A multimedia card is a portable (easily carried from one place to another) storage device the size of a postage stamp. It is used in mobile phones and digital cameras for storing data. It can be easily removed and used for transfer of data to a computer. The multimedia card is inserted into the card reader and is connected to the computer through the Universal Serial Bus (USB) cable.

Multimedia card

Flash drive

A flash drive is a small, portable memory card that plugs into a computer's USB port. It functions as a portable hard drive that can be used for sharing and transferring data. It is small enough to be carried in a pocket. It can be plugged into any computer with a USB drive. It is easy to use.

A USB flash drive has a large storage capacity, generally in terms of gigabytes. It does not contain any internal moving parts. It is small in size and highly durable. A USB flash drive is also called a thumb drive, pen drive, key drive, or simply a USB drive.

Advantages of a flash drive

Flash drive

1. It is portable.

2. It has high capacity for data storage.

3. It is less likely to have data damage.

Disadvantages of a flash drive

1. It is more likely to be lost due to its small size.

Online data storage

Online data storage or internet data storage is a technology that allows people to store their data on the internet. It is an effective method of sharing data with others. Another advantage of online data storage is that it is easy to expand. Whenever you reach the maximum capacity limit, you can simply purchase additional space for storage. No additional hardware is required. Many websites like Google and Dropbox provide their users with this facility.

Specific applications of computers

Computers have become an important part of our lives. They are used in almost every industry such as banking, science and technology, and medicine. You will now learn about the different applications of computers.

Education

Computers are commonly used for teaching and learning. An efficient storage and effective presentation of information is made easy by computers. Any topic can be made more interesting by combining text with suitable audio-visual effects with the help of a computer.

Computers in a school

Children can also prepare project reports, assignments and presentations with the help of computers. Computers are used in libraries for keeping a track of the issue and return of books, catalogue of books available, etc.

Science and Technology

Computers are used for the collection and analysis of data, experiment and research processes, etc. Computers help in the prediction of natural disasters like earthquakes and volcanic eruptions, and people can be forewarned

Computers in science

to avoid casualties. Artificial satellites and spacecrafts are monitored and controlled with the help of computers.

Medicine

Computers are used extensively in the industry of medicine. These are used to maintain and process medical records of patients for future reference.

Computerised equipments are used for diagnostic tests, surgeries, etc. They are also helpful in monitoring the condition of patients.

Computers in medicine

Business

Computers are used to maintain files and databases. They are also used for communicating information to clients through video conferencing, PowerPoint presentations, etc. These can be used for maintaining records, generating bills in grocery shops, sending emails for faster communication, maintaining stocks in the inventory, etc.

Computers in business

Music

Computers are very useful for musicians. They can compose tunes and find the best settings automatically. Sounds of different instruments can be generated easily using computers.

Computers in music

Entertainment

Computers are used to make motion pictures with a lot of special effects. Special effects, such as a sequence of a battle, can be created using a computer.

It is now possible to make cartoon films much more quickly than in the past with the help of computer animation. Animation is a technique that gives a character the appearance of movement.

Computers in entertainment

Computers can also be used to modify the pictures to suit your requirements.

Multimedia

Multimedia is a computer-based interactive communication process. It is a medium with multiple content forms such as text, graphics, sound, animation, video and still images integrated together. An example of multimedia is a web page about a sports match that includes text regarding the various players along with match commentary and videos of some replay actions.

Computers in multimedia

Multimedia applications

Multimedia is a very effective communication tool. It is used:

1. in business, as a presentation and sales tool
2. in homes, for entertainment and games
3. in education, for teaching and training
4. in public places, for advertising, spreading information, etc.

Limitations of computers

The following are some of the limitations of working with computers.

Garbage in, garbage out: Though computers are programmed to work efficiently, fast and accurately, they are programmed by humans to do so. Without a program, the computer is nothing. Computers only follow the instructions given. If the instructions given are inaccurate, then their processing and the output generated will also be inaccurate.

No decision making power: A computer cannot take decisions on its own. It only does tasks it is instructed to do.

No self-intelligence: A computer is able to do work which is not possible for humans. A computer is used to do difficult, risky and dangerous work where precision is needed. But it does not have any intelligence of its own. It only works according to the instructions given.

ACTIVITY

Match the boxes by coloring them alike.

1.	Hard disk	a.	Web camera
2.	Short term memory	b.	Secondary memory
3.	Looks like a TV	c.	Printer
4.	Used for video chatting	d.	Monitor
5.	Prints on paper	e.	RAM

GLOSSARY

ALU Stands for Arithmetic Logic Unit. It does mathematical and logical calculations.

Bytes A unit used to denote the storage capacity of a computer memory.

CU Stands for Control Unit. It controls the flow of information in the system.

MU Stands for Memory Unit. It holds the processed or unprocessed data.

RAM Stands for Random Access Memory. It stores the data temporarily and is called as volatile memory.

ROM Stands for Read Only Memory. It stores data permanently and is called non-volatile memory.

Visual Display Unit The computer monitor.

YOU ARE HERE

1

1. Input devices help to feed data or instructions into the computer.
2. The keyboard is an input device which operates like a typewriter. It has many additional keys.
3. The mouse is another input device. It is also known as a pointing device. The most common type of computer mouse is an optical mouse.
4. Output devices give the result or the information. The most commonly used output devices are computer monitors, printers, plotters and speakers.
5. Once information has been sent to a computer by one of the input devices, it is processed by the CPU.
6. The memory unit is the storage area of a computer. The computer has a large storage capacity. This capacity is measured in terms of bytes.
7. Primary memory is also called internal memory. It is the main area where data is stored in the computer.
8. Secondary memory is also called external memory. Here the data is stored on a long-term basis.
9. Computers are used in many areas like education, science, business, music, entertainment and multimedia.
10. A computer can only work based on the instructions given to it. It does not have decision-making capacity and does not have an intelligence of its own.

A. Give full forms of the following.

1. ALU

2. VDU

3. CU

4. RAM

5. ROM

6. LCD

7. LED

8. GB

9. MU

10. CD

B. Solve the crossword using the hints given below:

Across

2. It does mathematical and logical calculations in a computer.

3. It gives the output on paper.

6. It is a unit of the computer memory.

Down

1. These are stacked on a cylindrical rod in a hard disk.

4. It is temporary in nature.

5. It is permanent in nature.

6. It is used to start the operating system in a computer.

C. Fill in the blanks with the correct word.

| output | pointing | permanent | speaker | CPU | volatile |

1. The joystick and mouse are .... devices.
2. The .... is also known as the 'brain of a computer'.
3. The printer and speakers are .... devices.
4. ROM is .... in nature.
5. RAM is also called .... memory.
6. A .... is an output device that generates sound waves.

D. True or false?

1. Each key is expressed in terms of a bit.
2. Multimedia is a computer-based interactive communication process.
3. A flash drive is a portable storage device about the size of a postage stamp.
4. A Blu-ray disc stores a minimum of 4.7 GB of data while a DVD stores up to 25 GB.

E. Give one word for the following.

1. It operates like a typewriter, but has many additional keys. ....
2. It uses light to detect the movement of the mouse. ....
3. A set of lines of different thicknesses that represent a number. ....
4. Another name for Visual Display Unit. ....
5. A device that prints pictures on paper, based on the commands received from a computer. ....
6. A circular magnetic disc enclosed in a square or a rectangular shaped plastic body. ....

F. Answer the following questions.

1. What is secondary memory? Give any three examples.
2. BIOS is contained in ROM and not in RAM. Can you guess why?

3. Give one similarity and one difference between a Digital Versatile Disc and a Blu-ray disc.
4. Describe the difference between impact and non-impact printers. Give an example of each.
5. Explain briefly the different types of computer memory.
6. List the different uses of multimedia.
7. Paul is trying to save the folder of his family album of 1 GB on a CD. He is unable to do so. Can you guess why? Suggest an appropriate storage device.

LAB WORK

A. In the school lab, find out the different input and output devices available. Make a list of these in MS Word. Find a picture of each type of device, and write down one use for it.

B. Storage devices are used to store our data for future use. Use the internet to make a list of at least five of the latest storage devices available. Write a few lines about each.

PROJECT WORK

Work in groups. Each group selects a specific department of the school, for example, Accounts, Transport, Examination or HR. Each group will visit their chosen department and interview its members to find out what they use computers for in their jobs. Make a report in MS Word about the findings and share it with rest of the class.

I am a famous American scientist who is known as 'the father of the internet'. I was born in the USA on June 23, 1943.

I won the A. M. Turing Award, the highest honour in Computer Science.

I also worked extensively on internet working, including the design and implementation of the internet's basic communication protocols, TCP/IP.

I am well-known for my pioneering work on networking.

I am ....

Using Windows

SNAP RECAP

1. What is a Windows desktop?

2. What are icons?

3. What is a Taskbar?

4. What is the Recycle Bin?

5. Where is the Start button located?

LEARNING OBJECTIVES

You will learn about:

- setting the background and the screen saver of the desktop
- setting the date and time
- files and folders
- creating, copying, moving and deleting a file
- the accessories – Calculator, Notepad, Paint, WordPad, Media Player

Introduction

You have learnt about Windows as the most commonly used Graphical User Interface (GUI) operating system. The GUI provides a way to interact with the computer through graphics, like icons, drop down menus, buttons and scroll bars. An operating system is a system software that is necessary for a computer to function.

When the computer is switched on, the operating system is loaded onto the computer's memory. It remains there until the power is on.

In this chapter, you will learn more about the Windows 7 operating system. For Windows 10 updates, go to the end of the chapter.

Desktop background

The desktop background is the background image that appears on the desktop. It is similar to a table cloth with designs that you use to decorate the table top.

These designs can be taken from the list of options already available or can be created in Paint. You may also use photographs stored in the computer as a desktop background. These backgrounds are also called **Wallpapers**.

Steps to create a desktop background

If you wish to create a new desktop background, you may create a file in Paint.

1. Select **Start** ⟹ **All Programs** ⟹ **Accessories** ⟹ **Paint**.

2. Create your own design in the Paint window.

Drawing in the Paint window

3. Click on the **Paint** button drop-down list and select the **Set as desktop background** option.

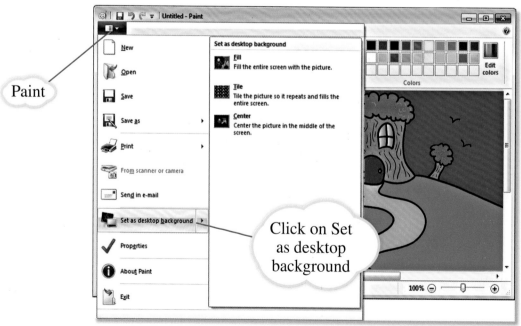

Selecting the desktop background

When you save a picture created in Paint you must give it a name for it to be used as the desktop background.

4. The image is displayed on the desktop as a desktop background.

Steps to change a desktop background

1. Right-click on the desktop. Click on the **Personalize** option in the shortcut menu.

Changing the desktop background using shortcut menu

FACT FILE

Windows 7 also gives options to choose from some preset themes. These include the Desktop Background, Window Color, Screen Saver and Sounds.

2. The **Personalization** window appears

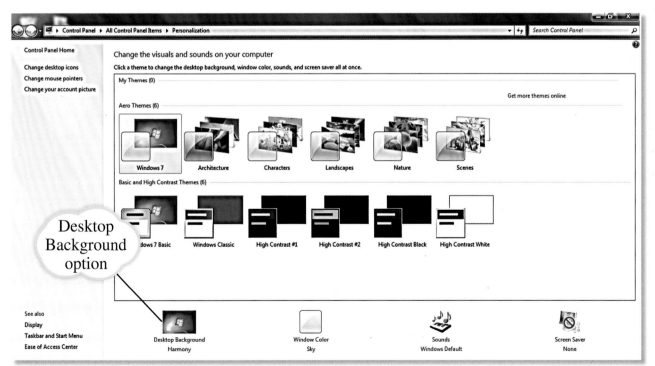

Personalization window

3. Click on the **Desktop Background** option. The **Choose your desktop background** window appears.

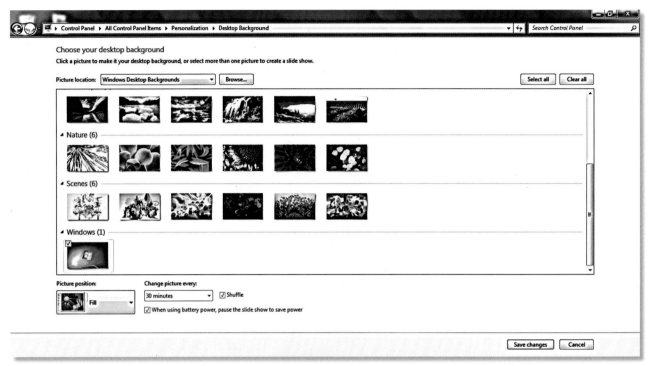

Desktop Background window

4. Select the background you want from the given list.
5. Double-click on the image or click on **Save changes**. You will return to the **Personalization** window.
6. Click on the **Close** button and the selected background will be seen on the desktop.

Screen Saver

A Screen saver is the image that you see when the computer is left idle (without you pressing any keys or moving the mouse) for some time. The screen saver disappears as soon as you click the mouse or press any key.

You can select screen savers from already stored templates in Windows or create new screen savers. The idle time after which the screen saver will be displayed can also be changed.

Steps to use a screen saver

1. Right-click on the desktop.
2. Select the **Personalize** option from the shortcut menu.

3. The **Personalization** window appears.

4. Click on the **Screen Saver** option. The **Screen Saver Settings** dialog box appears.

5. Select the screen saver of your choice from the Screen saver drop-down list.

Personalization window

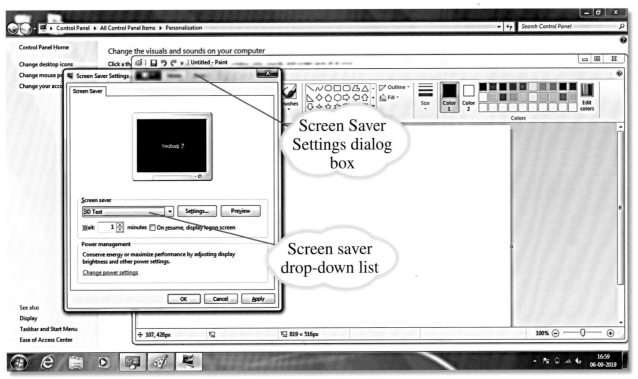

Specifying details for screen saver

6. You can also specify the time after which the screen saver should appear in the **Wait** box and tick the **On resume, display logon screen** checkbox.

7. Click **OK** or **Apply**.

8. Close the **Personalization** window by clicking the **Close** button.

TRY THIS

In the **Screen Saver Settings** dialog box, select 3D Text as your screen saver. Click on **Settings...** and you can write a message to yourself as your screen saver!

A. Create a logo for your school. Use it as the desktop background.

B. Change the screen saver of your desktop.

You can also access the Personalization window by taking the following path:
Start ⟹ Control Panel ⟹ Personalization option.

Setting Date and Time

Every computer has a built-in calendar and clock. It keeps on working even if the computer is shut down. It is displayed on the right end of the taskbar. You can change the time and the date by clicking on it on the taskbar.

Click on the **Change date and time settings…** option. The **Date and Time** dialog box appears. Here you can change the date and time.

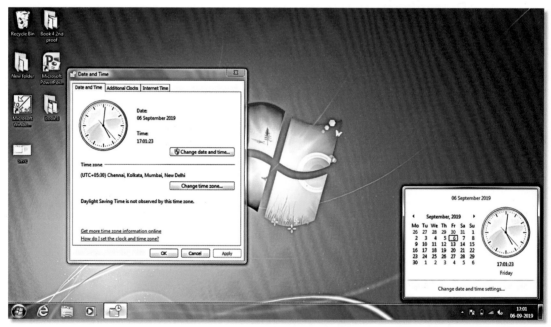

Date and Time dialog box

Windows Explorer

Windows Explorer works as a manager for the windows. It manages and organises files and folders. It is also known as the **File Manager**. You can delete, view, copy or move files and folders with the help of Windows Explorer.

To open Windows Explorer follow the steps given here.

1. Click on the **Start** button.
2. Select **All Programs**.
3. Click on **Accessories**.
4. Click on the **Windows Explorer** option. The **Windows Explorer** window appears, which is set to the **Library** view by default.

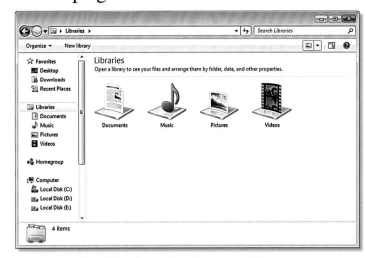

Opening Windows Explorer in Library view

Double-click on the **Computer** icon on the desktop to open **Windows Explorer** with **Computer** as the default view.

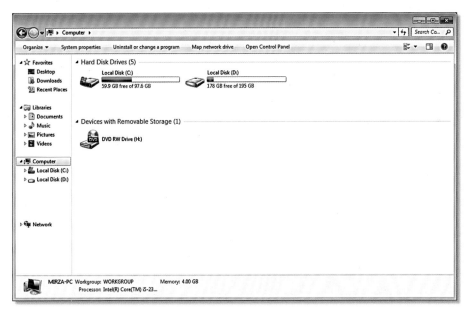

Windows Explorer in Computer view

You can also open Windows Explorer by clicking on the Windows Explorer icon on the taskbar.

Files

A file is a collection of related information. There are different types of files depending on the type of information they contain. For example, image files, program files, text files and music files, etc.

Each file is given a name, known as the **File name**. It is useful for identifying the file. Every file has two names – a *primary name* and a *secondary name*.

Primary name: The first name of a file. It can be any name given by the user.

Secondary name: The extension of the file like .docx, .bmp, .xlsx. This name is given by the program in which it is created. It may vary with the application used. For example, if the file is created in MS Word 2010, then it is a .docx file.

Folders

Folders are used to classify files in a computer. A collection of related files can be grouped in a common folder. You can name a folder just as a file is named. A folder can contain files as well as other folders.

The folders are also known as **directories**. Usually, a folder is represented by the icon shown here.

Folder icon

Inside Windows Explorer

All the stored data in a computer can be accessed in Windows Explorer. You can view, create new, copy, delete or move files and folders with the help of Windows Explorer. The window is divided into two panes, the left and the right.

In the left pane of this window, also known as the navigation pane, there is a directory tree. It contains the list of folders and subfolders in the system.

The right pane of the window shows the contents of the folder currently selected in the left pane. Both files and folders contained in the main folder are displayed. Depending on the type of view activated, you will see different types of information regarding the files and folders. For example, you can see the name, size, type and date of last modification of each file and folder.

Click on the **Change your view** drop-down list in the upper-right corner of the window. Try the different options given.

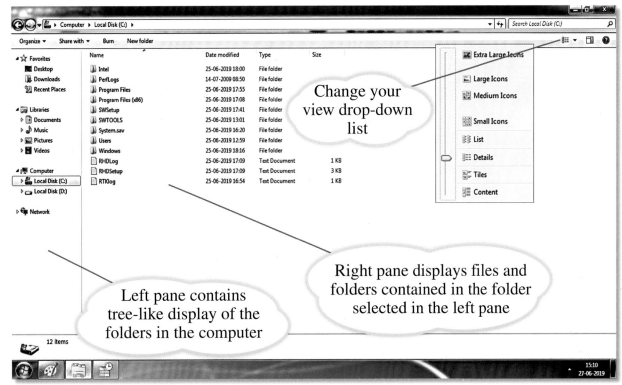

Inside Windows Explorer

Selecting files and folders

To select a single file or folder, click on it. Any operation you perform will then apply to the selected file or folder.

To select multiple files and folders in a sequence, click on the first file/folder and then click on the last one while keeping the **Shift** key pressed.

To select multiple files and folders that are not placed together, select the first file/folder and continue to select others while keeping the **Ctrl** key pressed.

Creating a new folder

1. Open **Windows Explorer**.
2. In the left pane of Windows Explorer, click the folder where a new folder needs to be created. For example, click on **Documents** in **Libraries**.
3. Click on the **New folder** option in the **Menu** bar.
4. A new folder with the name **New folder** appears in the right pane. Give this new folder a name and press the **Enter** key.

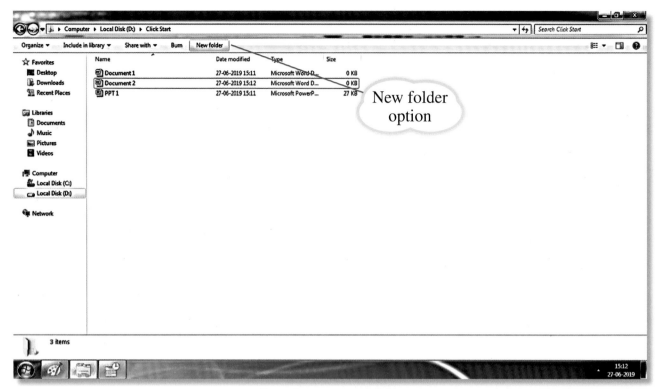

Creating a new folder

Deleting a file or a folder

To delete a file or folder follow the steps given below.

1. In the right pane of Windows Explorer, select the file or folder to be deleted.
2. Click on **Organize** drop-down list ⟹ **Delete** option. The **Delete Folder** dialog box appears. Click **Yes** to confirm deletion.

 OR

1. Right-click on the folder required to be deleted.
2. Select **Delete** from the shortcut menu.
3. The **Delete Folder** dialog box appears. Click **Yes** to confirm deletion.

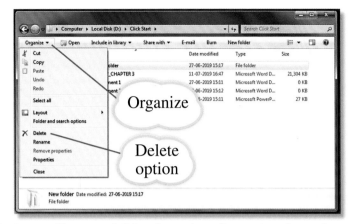

Deleting a file or a folder by using Organize drop-down list

Copying a file or folder

Copying a file or folder means making a copy of the original file in another location, without removing it from its original location.

1. Select the file or folder in its respective location.
2. In Windows Explorer, click on the **Organize** drop-down list ⟹ **Copy** option.

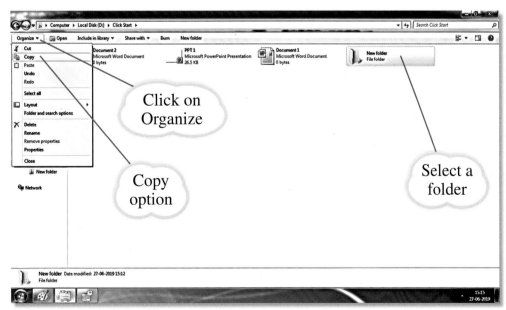

Copying a folder

3. Select the destination folder either from the navigation pane or locate it through the Address bar.

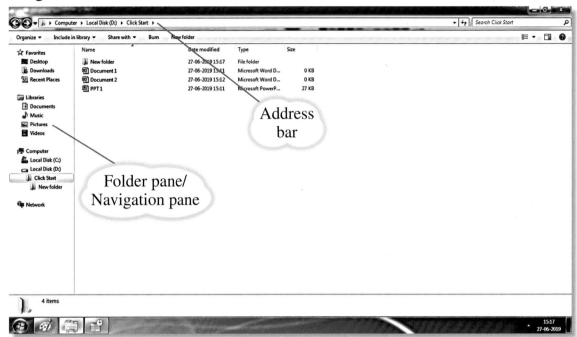

Selecting the destination folder

4. In the chosen location, click on the **Organize** drop-down list ⟹ **Paste** option.

Right-click the mouse in the destination folder. Select the **Copy** or **Paste** option from the shortcut menu.

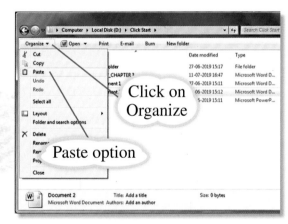

Pasting a folder

Moving a file or folder to another folder

1. In Windows Explorer, select the file or folder to be moved.

2. Click on the **Organize** drop-down list ⟹ **Cut** option.

3. Select the destination folder from the navigation pane.

4. Click on the **Organize** drop-down list ⟹ **Paste** option in the destination folder to move the file or folder.

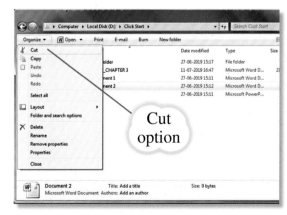

Using Organize option

You can also move the cut file or folder into a new folder.

1. Click on the **New folder** in the **Menu** bar.
2. Open the folder and then select **Paste** from the **Organize** drop-down list.

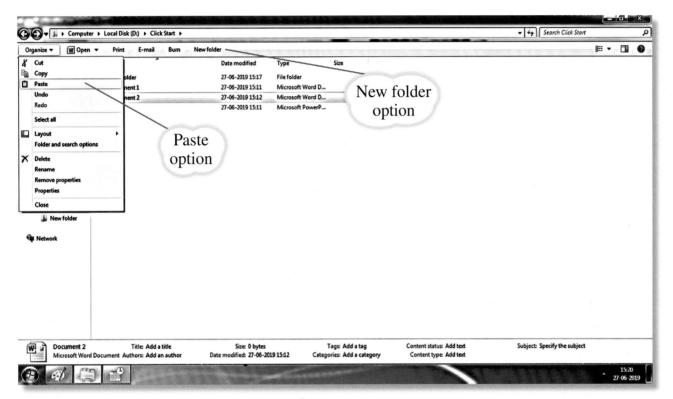

Using the organize option

Changing the name of a file or a folder

1. Select the file or folder.
2. Right-click on the mouse.
3. Select **Rename** from the shortcut menu.
4. The name of the selected file or folder will be highlighted with the pointer blinking inside the name box. Write the new name.

5. Press **Enter** key or click outside the file or the folder.

A. Go to your computer and create the folders given in the hierarchy below.

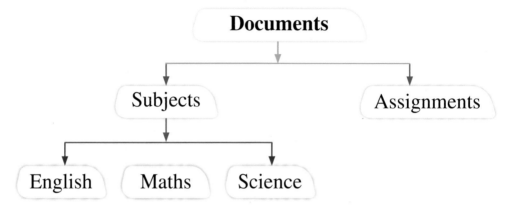

Documents

Subjects   **Assignments**

English   **Maths**   **Science**

B. Delete the Science folder.

C. Move the Maths folder into the Assignments folder.

D. Create an Assignment file within the English folder.

E. Copy the English Assignment file, which you have just created, and paste it in the Assignments folder.

Accessories

Windows have a number of standard applications referred to as Accessories. Some of these applications such as Calculator, Paint, WordPad and Notepad are frequently used.

These applications are simple and easy to use.

To access any of these applications, say Calculator, click on **Start ⟹ All Programs ⟹ Accessories ⟹ Calculator**.

Selecting Calculator and an already opened Calculator window

Calculator

By default, Calculator looks like a real pocket calculator. It has number keys, memory keys and standard maths operations. You can use the Calculator program with the help of the keyboard or mouse.

The **View** menu allows you to use different programming capabilities like a scientific, programmer and statistical calculator. Apart from using the different types of calculators, the View menu provides the user with a few other useful features. The **Date calculation** option allows you to calculate the difference between two dates in terms of years, months, weeks and days. The **Unit conversion** option converts values from one unit of measurement to another. The **Digit Grouping** option groups the numbers typed on the calculator based on the International system of numeration.

TRY THIS

To do a scientific calculation, select
View menu
↓
Scientific option

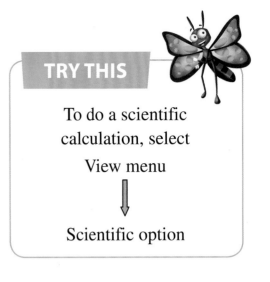

Conversion of values using calculator

The **Edit** menu allows the user to copy values from the calculator and paste in another location and vice versa.

Notepad

Notepad is a basic text-editing program in Windows. You can create, edit and print a document file with simple formatting features. You can also scribble notes and important points and save them for future references.

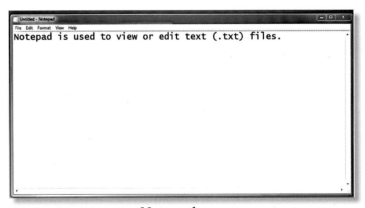

Notepad

You can work on only one document at a time in Notepad. You can create, edit and save a Notepad file as a plain text file (.txt).

WordPad

WordPad is a rich text-editing program. It is capable of doing much more than Notepad but compared to MS Word it has fewer features. A file created in WordPad can be a plain text file (.txt), a rich text format file (.rtf), a word document file (.docx) or an open document text file (.odt).

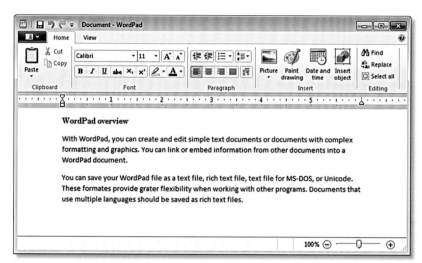

WordPad

The formatting features are more advanced than Notepad - for example, you can insert an image in a document file.

TRY THIS

In WordPad, right-click on an option in the Ribbon and select **Add to Quick Access Toolbar**. The option will then be added to the **Quick Access Toolbar**.

Paint

Paint is a drawing and painting program in Windows. Pictures that are drawn or edited in Paint are called **bitmaps**. They are stored as a grid of small dots, called **pixels**. Paint consists of drawing tools that help to create pictures. It also

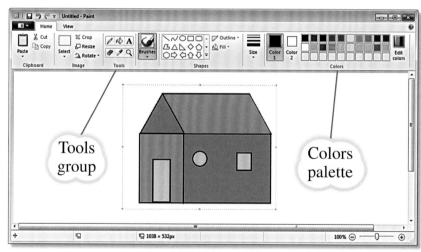

Paint window

includes a Colors palette that allows the user to choose both the foreground and background color of the picture.

A. Draw a few cartoon characters in Paint. Save the file.

B. Write a letter in Notepad to the headteacher to organise a school celebration on New Year's Eve.

C. Insert the image created in Paint into WordPad with a few lines about it. Save the file as My Work.rtf.

D. In your notebook, list the differences between the Notepad and the WordPad applications.

Windows Media Player

Windows also has several entertainment software applications. One such application is Windows Media Player.

You can listen to audio files and watch videos with the help of Windows Media Player. You can also use it to play CDs and DVDs. This software allows you to copy songs from CDs on to your computer. It is a multimedia application available in various versions.

How to Open Windows Media Player

1. Click on the **Start** button.
2. Select **All Programs**.
3. Click on **Windows Media Player**.

Every Windows Media Player comes with some default music stored in the **Sample Music** folder of the computer.

Windows Media Player

GLOSSARY

Accessories   The set of standard applications in Windows.

Active window   The window currently being used.

Bitmaps   Pictures drawn or edited in Paint.

Desktop background   The list of images and designs used to decorate the desktop.

File   A collection of related information.

Inactive window   A window which is open but is not in use.

Screen Saver   The moving images that start after a specified amount of time when the computer is not being used.

YOU ARE HERE

2

1. The desktop background is the list of images and designs used to decorate the desktop.

2. The Screen Saver displays the moving images that start automatically when the computer is idle for a specified amount of time.

3. Every program is in the form of a window with Title bar, Menu bar, Scroll bars and control buttons like Maximize, Minimize and Close.

4. Every computer has a built-in Calendar and Clock. It keeps on working even if the computer is shut down. It is displayed on the right end of the taskbar.

5. A file is a collection of related information. There are different types of files depending on the type of information they contain.

6. Folders are used to classify the files on a computer. A collection of related files can be grouped in a common folder.

7. Windows has a manager called Windows Explorer. It manages the files and folders. Windows Explorer is also known as the File Manager. You can use it to delete, view, copy or move files and folders.

8. Calculator, Paint, Notepad and WordPad are some of the accessories in Windows.

EXERCISE

A. Fill in the blanks.

1. .... is the image that you see when the computer is left idle for some time.
2. .... is a collection of related information.
3. A window which is open but is not in use is called ....
4. Windows has a manager called ....
5. In order to set a Screen Saver, you need to open the .... window.
6. .... is a basic text editor program in Windows.

B. True or false?

1. The primary name of the file may vary with the application used.

2. Folders are also known as directories.

3. Pictures that are drawn or edited in Paint are called bitmaps.

4. WordPad is a basic text-editing program in Windows.

5. Windows Media Player is a multimedia application.

C. Rewrite the un jumbled words.

1. ONDWISW

2. EFLI

3. ODFREL

4. PNETAOD

5. ORCCLLAUAT

6. PDTEOKS

D. Write the steps to create your own desktop background using Paint.

1. ....
2. ....
3. ....
4. ....

E. Answer the following questions.

1. What is the difference between primary and secondary names of a file?
2. What is the purpose of the Start button?
3. How do you change the date and time in Windows?
4. What is the difference between copying a file and moving a file?
5. What is the use of different menus available in Calculator?

LAB WORK

A. Create a folder named CLASSMATES in the Documents folder and then follow the instructions below.

1. Select the folder and create a text file within it. Name it after one of your classmates. Double-click on this file and write at least three lines about your classmate. Repeat the same steps for other classmates.
2. Create another folder named MY FRIENDS in the Documents folder. Copy into the folder the files of those classmates who are your close friends.
3. In the CLASSMATES folder, delete the file(s) whose name begins with the letter 'A'.
4. Move the file(s) to the desktop if the letter 'S' appears in its name.

B. Follow the steps given below.
1. Create a folder with your name on the desktop using the shortcut menu.
2. Cut and paste the folder in the Documents folder.
3. Add a few documents and pictures created by you to the folder.

C. Create a picture of a traffic light in Paint and save it with the name: traffic.bmp. Set this picture as a desktop background.

PROJECT WORK

Open WordPad. Create a new document. Type a list of all the Windows Accessories. Write five sentences about any two of the Accessories which you think are most useful to you. Add relevant icons/pictures related to the Accessories you have selected. Save your file in the Documents folder with the name: Chapter2Project.docx.

Windows 10
Updates

1. Windows 10 operating system is the successor of version Windows 8.1 and was launched in 2015. It has combined features of both Windows 7 and 8 to make it more user-friendly.

2. For setting the **Screen Saver**, right-click on the **Desktop** and select the **Personalize** option. It opens the window given below.

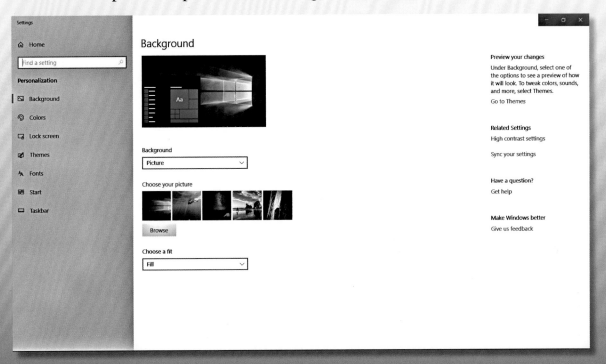

Then, select **Lock screen** ⟹ **Screen Saver Settings** to set the Screen Saver of your choice.

3. Windows Explorer is known as **File Explorer** in Windows 10. To open File Explorer, click on **Start ⟹ File Explorer** or you can use the shortcut keys: **Windows + E**. The layout of the File Explorer in Windows 10 is similar to the previous versions of Windows with minor changes.

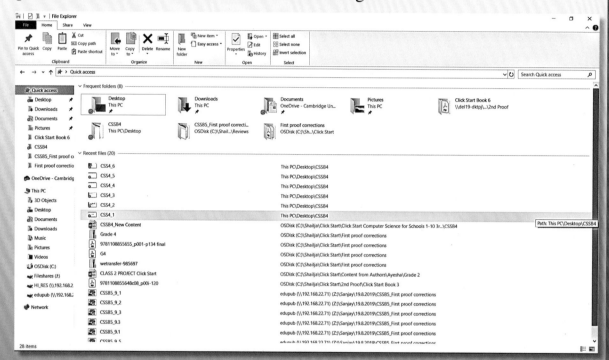

4. The Accessories folder is no longer included in the Windows Start menu. To find programs such as Calculator and Paint, you must now open the Windows Start menu and click the 'All apps' option to see the list of programs. Or you can just search for the program you want by typing the name into the Windows search box next to Start.

MS Word 2010 – Formatting Text

SNAP RECAP

1. What is the Quick Access Toolbar? What commands are accessible through this toolbar?
2. What are the different components of the MS Word 2010 window?
3. How do you change the case of already typed text?
4. How do you find a particular word in a document and replace it with another word?

LEARNING OBJECTIVES

You will learn about:

- changing fonts, font sizes, font styles and font color
- highlighting text
- applying borders and shadings
- text alignment – centre, left, right and 'justify'
- bullets and numbering

Introduction

Formatting is organising or arranging text in a word processor, such as MS Word, according to a chosen pattern. It helps in changing the appearance of the text. This is done by using different fonts, colors, sizes and styles. Every software package has predefined settings. These are called **default settings**. Formatting helps you to change the default settings of the computer according to your choice.

In this chapter, you will learn about different ways to format text. When you are formatting text, you don't need to highlight the entire text. Placing the cursor anywhere in the text enables you to format that part.

Similarly, you can format an entire paragraph. Once the settings of the text in the paragraph are selected, subsequent paragraphs will have the same format unless the format is changed.

Fonts

Formatting is the process of applying font style, characteristics, colors, etc. to a text or a paragraph. In other words, it is the way the text appears on a page. The default font in MS Word 2010 is 'Calibri'. The default font size is 11 points. Therefore, any new word document in MS Word 2010 would have the text in 'Calibri', 11 points by default.

In MS Word 2010, the formatting of the text document can be done by:

1. Selecting different options given in the **Font** group of the **Home** tab.

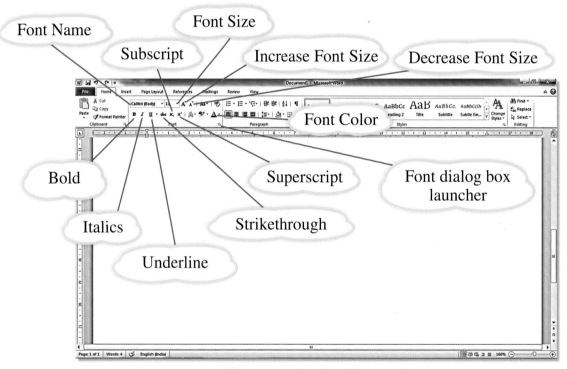

Font group in the Home tab

2. We can also select different options through the **Font** dialog box launcher in the **Font** group of the **Home** tab.

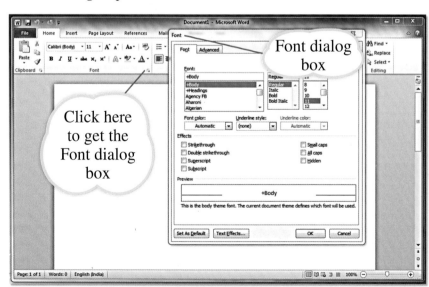

Using the Font dialog box

Font Name

A font is a set of letters and symbols in a particular design and size. Each font has a name. Some examples of fonts are listed here.

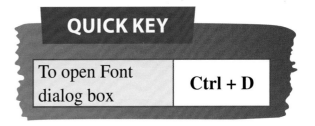
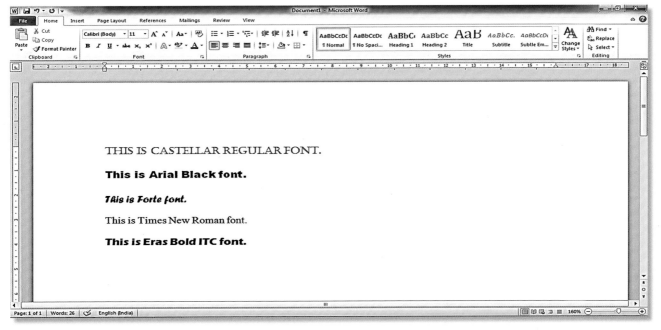

A few examples of fonts

Font Size

The size of the text is called the **font size**. It is measured in points. There are 72 points. A few examples are given on the next page.

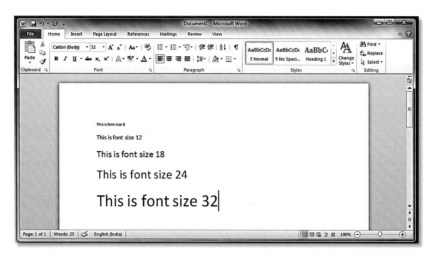

Examples of font sizes

Font Style

The way in which a character is emphasised is called its **font style**. The most common styles are bold, italic and underline.

Bold **B**

Bold text is printed darker than normal text so that words and phrases stand out on a page. It is often used for titles and headings.

Italic *I*

Italic text is slanted. It is mostly used for emphasis. It is sometimes used for headings and also for representing scientific names.

Underline **U**

Underlined text has a line under it. In the **Font** dialog box, you can select the **Underline style** from the drop-down list. From the **Underline color** drop-down list, you can select the line color. It is also used to emphasise the text. It is sometimes used for the title of a document.

You can also choose the **More Underlines…** option from the **Underline** drop-down list. A **Font** dialog box opens from where more styles for underlining the text can be chosen. Normal text is the default style for a document.

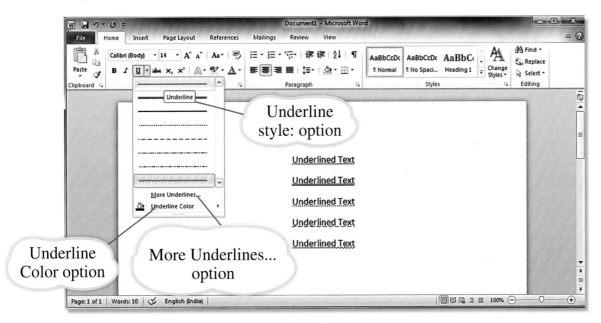

Selecting the underline option

ACTIVITY

Write a paragraph of five sentences on "I love computers because..." using the font Comic Sans MS, size: 18. Use different colors for each sentence.

Superscript x^2

Superscript reduces the size of the text and raises it to the top of the current line.

For example, 'today is 5th January'. Here, 'th' after the digit 5 is a superscript.

Subscript x_2

Subscript is a text style that reduces the size of the text and lowers it to the bottom of the current line.

For example, 'the chemical formula of water is H_2O'. Here the base '2' is a subscript.

Font Color A

This is used to change the color of the text to emphasise headings, subheadings and other text.

Avoid using too many bright colors in a single document.

Highlighting text

You can highlight the text in a Word document with different colors. It is usually done to draw attention to important facts in the text. The steps to highlight the text are:

1. Click on the **Text Highlight Color** drop-down list in the **Font** group of the **Home** tab. You may also choose different colors for highlighting.
2. The cursor changes to a highlighter pen. Move the pen over the text that has to be highlighted.
3. To remove the highlight from the text, select the **No Color** option from the **Text Highlight Color** drop-down list.

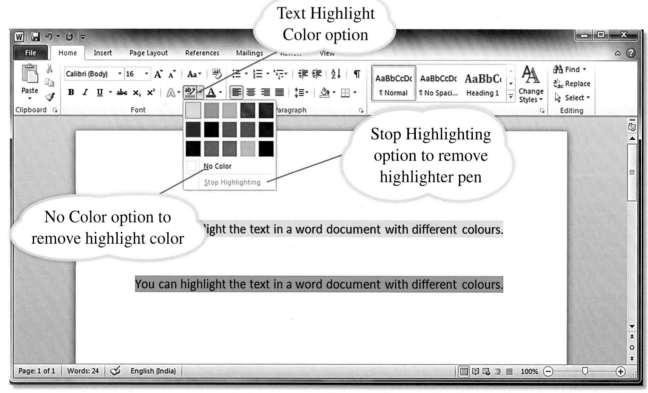

Highlighting text with a different color

Borders and shading

Follow these steps to apply borders and shading effects to the text.

1. Select the text where the border and shading effect is to be applied.
2. Click on the **Bottom Border** drop-down list in the **Paragraph** group of the **Home** tab.
3. Select the **Borders and Shading...** option in the drop-down list. The **Borders and Shading** dialog box appears.

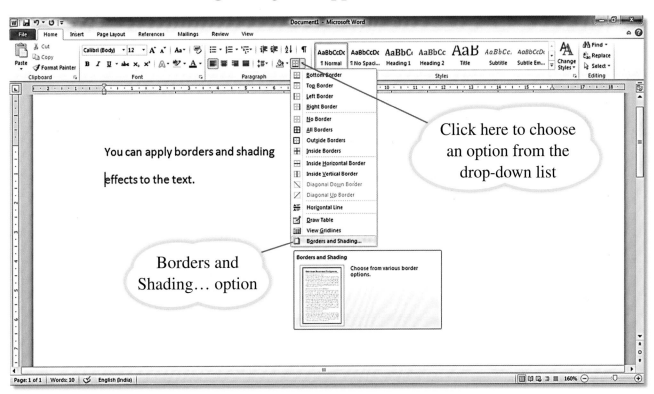

Selecting borders and shading

4. Click on the **Borders** tab and choose the box style from the **Setting** section.

Click on **None** to remove the borders.

5. You can also select the style, color and width of the border lines from the **Style**, **Color** and **Width** sections, respectively.

   The **Preview** section shows how the border will look when applied to the text.

6. Go to the **Apply to** drop-down list and select **Paragraph**.

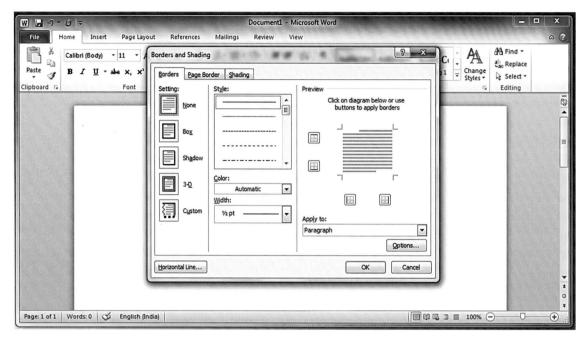

Borders and shading dialog box

7. Click on the **Shading** tab, select the color for shading from the **Fill** drop-down list.

8. You can also select the shading style and color using the **Style** and **Color** options respectively in the **Patterns** section.

   The **Preview** corner shows how the shading effect will look when applied to the text.

9. Click on the **OK** button to apply the border and shading effects to the selected text.

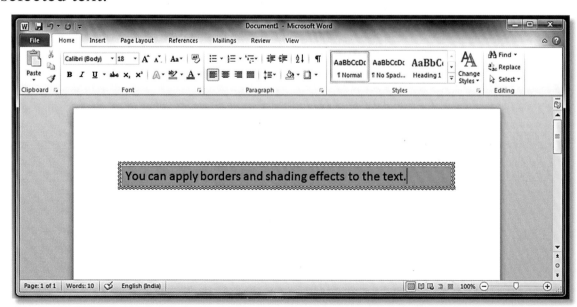

Text with border and shading effects

Complete the activity using MS Word 2010 and following the instructions below.

1. Create a slogan 'Save the Environment'.

2. Add a suitable heading. Set the font name 'Algerian' with font size 18 and font color blue.

3. Apply the italic style to the slogan. Set the font name 'Bookman Old Style' with font size 14 and font color green.

Text alignment

Text alignment refers to the text layout and the document margins. There are four types of alignments. These are discussed here. It is very simple to change the alignment of text. Follow these steps to change the alignment.

1. Select the text that you wish to align.

2. Click on the appropriate alignment button in the **Paragraph** group of the **Home** tab.

3. For example, to align text to the left, select the text and click on the **Align Text Left** option.

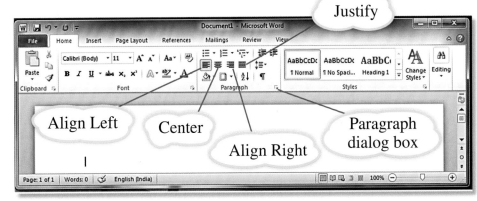

Options for text alignment

Align Left

This is the default alignment. In this type of alignment, the text is aligned from the left and ragged (not aligned) from the right edge.

Align Right

In this type of text alignment, the text is aligned from the right edge and ragged from the left side.

Center

This alignment aligns the text centrally and leaves it ragged at the right and left edges.

Justify

In this alignment, the text is aligned both to the right and to the left margins, adding extra space between words as necessary. Therefore, neither the left nor the right edge of the text appears ragged.

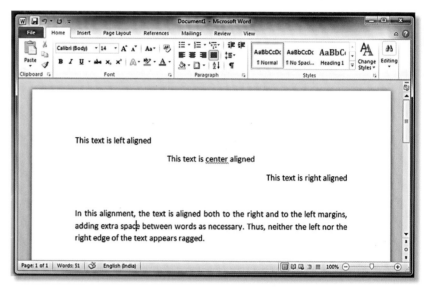

Different types of text alignment

Complete the following activity.

1. Write ten sentences on the topic 'My City'.
2. Write the date on the top of the page. Align it to the right.
3. Put your topic as the heading in the centre of page.
4. Align the sentences about your city as Justified.

Bullets and numbering

Bullets and numbered lists are used to present information in the form of points. By default, MS Word 2010 uses a simple black dot as a bullet.

In a bulleted text, each item of a list is added by using the **Enter** key. This creates a new point. Each item begins with a symbol called a bullet.

In order to display an unordered list, bullets (•) are used. If a document requires an ordered list, then the number list is used.

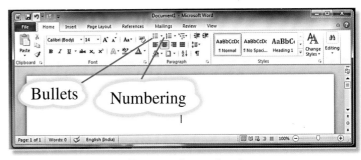

Bullets and numbering

Creating a bulleted or numbered list as you type

1. To start a numbered list, type '1.' and press the **Space Bar** or **Tab** key. To start a bulleted list, type * (asterisk) and press the **Space Bar** or **Tab** key.
2. Now type the text.
3. Press the **Enter** key to add the next item to the list. MS Word 2010 automatically inserts the next number or bullet.

Creating a bulleted or numbered list for an existing text

1. Select the text or paragraph to which numbering or bullets are to be applied.
2. Select the style of the bullets from the **Bullets** drop-down list ⠿▾ or the style of numbering from the **Numbering** drop-down list ⠿▾ in the **Paragraph** group of the **Home** tab.

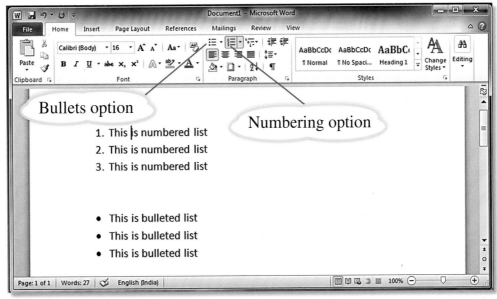

Bullets and numbering drop-down lists

Explore new bullet styles using the **Symbol…** and **Picture…** buttons in the **Define New Bullet…** option of the **Bullets** drop-down list. You can also add effects to your bullet styles using the **Font…** option. Similarly, explore new numbering styles using the **Define New Number Format…** option in the **Numbering** drop-down list.

QUICK KEY

To make text Bold	**Ctrl + B**	To clear formatting	**Ctrl + Space bar**
To make text Italics	**Ctrl + I**	To Left Align a paragraph	**Ctrl + L**
To Underline text	**Ctrl + U**	To Right Align a paragraph	**Ctrl + R**
To apply Superscript	**Ctrl + Shift + =**	To Center Align a paragraph	**Ctrl + E**
To apply Subscript	**Ctrl + =**	To Justify text in a paragraph	**Ctrl + J**

ACTIVITY

Mary has prepared a project report on 'Biofriendly Chemicals'. She wants to make her project report look impressive. What commands should she use to make the following changes in her report?

1. Make the text aligned on both sides   …………………………

2. Make the text a little darker   …………………………

3. Underline the text   …………………………

4. Raise the number to the power   …………………………

5. Write the base for a chemical formula (e.g. H_2O)   …………………………

6. Make the text slanted   …………………………

7. Write the heading in the centre   …………………………

8. Write the points using letters   …………………………

GLOSSARY

Bold   Darker printed text so that words and phrases stand out on a page.

Font name   The design/style of characters.

Font size   The size of characters.

Font style   The way in which a character is emphasised - the most common styles are bold, italics and underline.

Formatting text   The process of applying font style, colors, etc. to the text.

Italic text   Slanted text used for emphasis.

Superscript   A text style that reduces the size of the text and raises it to the top of the existing line.

Subscript   A text style that reduces the size of the text and lowers it to the bottom of the existing line.

Text alignment   Changing the layout of the text by changing the document margins.

Underline text   A line under the text that is mostly used for emphasis.

YOU ARE HERE

3

1. Formatting is organising or arranging text according to a selected pattern.
2. Font size is measured in points. There are 72 points to choose from.
3. Font color can be changed to emphasise specific text.
4. The Highlight button is used to highlight important text.
5. The highlight color can be changed as well as removed from the text.
6. Bullets are used to display an unordered list.
7. A numbered list is used when the order is important.

EXERCISE

A. State true or false.

1. The font is a type of alignment.

2. 'Justify' aligns the text both to the right and to the left margins, adding extra space between words as necessary.

3. Numbering is used to create an unordered list.

4. The process of applying font style, colors, etc. to the text is known as text formatting.

5. The default font name in MS Word 2010 is Times New Roman.

B. Match the following font styles.

1. *FONT*   a. Subscript

2. **FONT**   b. Underline text

3. FO$_{NT}$ c. Superscript

4. <u>FONT</u>   d. Bold

5. FO^{NT} e. Italic text

C. Write the shortcut keys for the following.

1. To Underline the text ....

2. To Right align a paragraph ....

3. To clear formatting ....

4. To apply Superscript ....

5. To Justify text in a paragraph ....

D. Identify and write the names of the options labelled below.

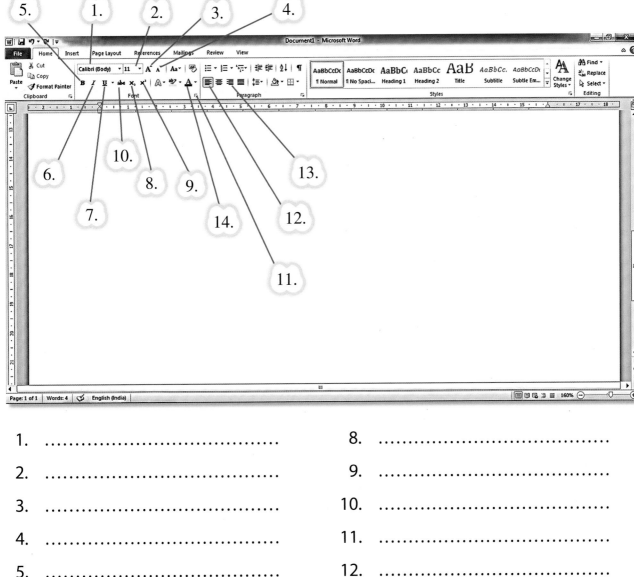

1. ....
2. ....
3. ....
4. ....
5. ....
6. ....
7. ....

8. ....
9. ....
10. ....
11. ....
12. ....
13. ....
14. ....

E. Answer the following questions.

1. What is text formatting?
2. Name the alignments available in MS Word 2010.
3. How can you change the alignment of the text?
4. Name any four formatting tools available on the Home tab.
5. Write the steps to create a bulleted list.

LAB WORK

A. Create a list of countries and their capitals. Format the text using an appropriate color scheme. Display the data in the form of bulleted points.

B. Write an article on different types of font styles available in MS Word 2010. Put an example of each style in the document. Apply borders and shading to your document.

C. Using bullets and numbering, make a list of the keyboard shortcuts you have learned in this chapter.

PROJECT WORK

Work in groups and select the project of your choice from the options given below.

1. Make a list of ten fonts and write ten sentences using these fonts – all the sentences should be in different font sizes.

2. Make a list of subjects and teachers. Use bullets and highlight each subject with a different color. This list of subject teachers should have an attractive border.

3. Write the steps for making lemonade. Use the numbering option and highlight each step with a different color. This whole process should be given an attractive border.

Fun with Tux Paint

SNAP RECAP

1. What is Tux Paint?
2. What is the difference between Tux Paint and Paint software?
3. What are the different drawing tools available in Tux Paint?
4. How do you open an existing file in Tux Paint?
5. How do you quit from Tux Paint?

LEARNING OBJECTIVES

You will learn about:

- using the Stamp tool
- using the Label tool
- opening a new Drawing Canvas
- setting up a slide show
- printing a picture in Tux Paint

Introduction

You have already learnt how to use the basic tools in Tux Paint to create drawings. In addition to those, you can also use stamps, create storyboards and run slide shows in Tux Paint. You can even choose canvasses of different kinds for your work.

In this chapter, you will learn the advanced features of Tux Paint that will make your drawings even better.

Using the Stamp tool

This a collection of rubber stamps and stickers. It allows you to add ready-made images to your pictures.

An outline image of the stamp is seen when the mouse is brought over the Drawing Canvas, telling the user about its size and location.

Multiple copies of the same stamp or of different stamps can be placed at different locations in the Drawing Canvas.

Different categories of stamps are available for use in the Selector pane of the Tux Paint window.

There are additional options in the Stamp tool which allow the user to flip the selected stamp vertically or create its mirror image.

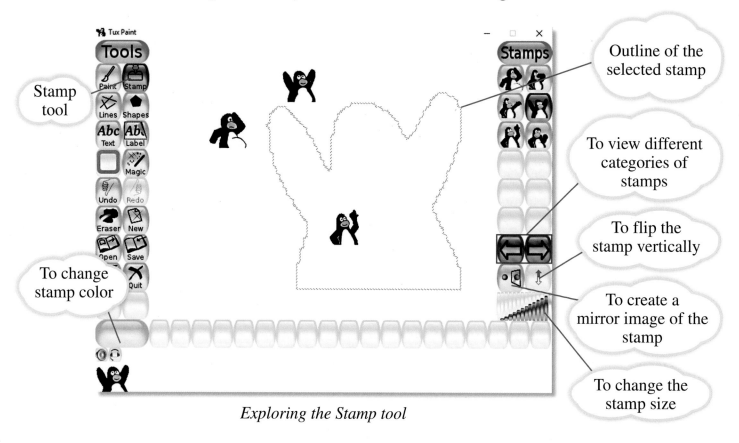

Exploring the Stamp tool

There is an option to change the stamp size. In some cases, the Colors palette in the lower part of the screen is active and allows the user to change the color of the stamp.

How to Add a Stamp

1. Click on the **Stamp** tool in the **Toolbar** pane. A list of stamps will appear in the **Selector** pane.

2. Move through the different categories of stamps available using the left and right arrow buttons in the **Selector** pane. Select the stamp you want.

3. Click on the appropriate tools in the **Selector** pane to increase or decrease the stamp size, to flip it vertically, to create its mirror image or to change its color in case the **Colors palette** is active.

5. Bring the cursor to the **Drawing Canvas**. An outline of the selected stamp will move with the movement of the mouse showing how and where the stamp will be placed.

6. Click on the left mouse button to place the stamp at the chosen location.

Creating a picture using the Stamp tool

TRY THIS

The sounds in Tux Paint can be disabled by pressing **Alt + S** (called muting) and can be re-enabled using the same combination.

Label Tool

The **Label tool** is used to type text in Tux paint. It can be used to write on any object or stamp.

In order to type, place the cursor on any part of the drawing and start typing. Use the Enter key to end the text. By using the selector button you can edit, move or change the style of the text.

Different categories of text styles are available for use in the Selector pane of the Tux Paint window.

There are additional options in the label tool which allow the user to flip the selected label format vertically. The text is available in varying sizes, which can be selected using the arrow keys.

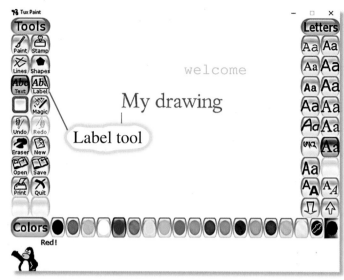

Using the Label tool

Opening a new Drawing Canvas

You can create new pictures in Tux Paint using the **New** tool. Tux Paint offers not only a blank, white canvas for drawing but also canvasses with different colors in the background, black-and-white outlines and 3-D photographs.

Follow these steps to open a new drawing canvas in Tux Paint:

1. Open the **Tux Paint** window.
2. Click on the **New** tool in the **Toolbar** pane.
3. A list of canvasses open. Scroll up and down using the arrows.
4. Select your chosen canvas and click on the **Open** button.

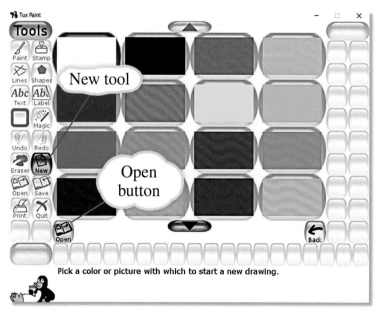

Using the New tool

FACT FILE

The black-and-white outlines and 3-D pictures used as canvas in Tux Paint are called **Starters**. On clicking **Save**, Tux Paint saves the changes made to the Starter as a separate file and does not overwrite the original.

Follow the instructions below in Tux Paint.

1. Use a black and white canvas outline. Now draw and color a 3D picture on the canvas.

2. Save the picture.

3. Add a stamp of your choice to the picture.

4. Save the new version of the file as a separate file.

Viewing pictures as a Slide Show

Pictures created in Tux Paint can also be viewed as a slide show. Follow these steps to watch a slide show of the pictures created.

1. Select the **Open** tool in the **Toolbar** pane.

2. A list of pictures created and saved in Tux Paint appear as thumbnails in the virtual **Picturebook**.

3. Click on the **Slides** button in the lower-left corner of the virtual **Picturebook**.

4. A new pane appears in the middle of the window containing pictures saved in Tux Paint. Click on the images in the sequence in which you want them to appear in the slide show. The images will be numbered accordingly.

Click on a selected image to remove it from the slide show. If no image is selected, then all the images will appear in the slide show.

5. Set the speed of slide change using the sliding scale next to the **Play** button.

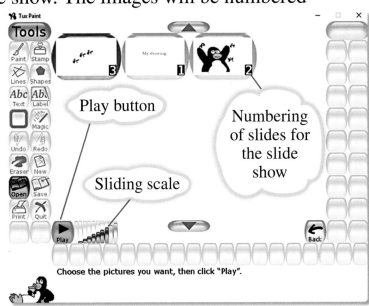

Preparing a slide show

6. Click on the **Play** button to start the slide show.

7. Slides change automatically after the selected time or you can click on the **Next** button to move to the next slide.

8. Click on the **Back** button to go back to the thumbnails.

With this feature, Tux Paint can also be used to create storyboards.

Printing a picture

The pictures created in Tux Paint can also be printed. Follow these steps to print a picture:

1. Click on the **Print** tool in the **Toolbar** pane.

2. A dialog box appears asking for your permission to print the opened picture. Click on the **Yes, print it!** option.

3. The **Print** dialog box appears. Select the printer connected to your computer in the **Select Printer** section and specify your printing preferences.

4. Click on the **Print** button.

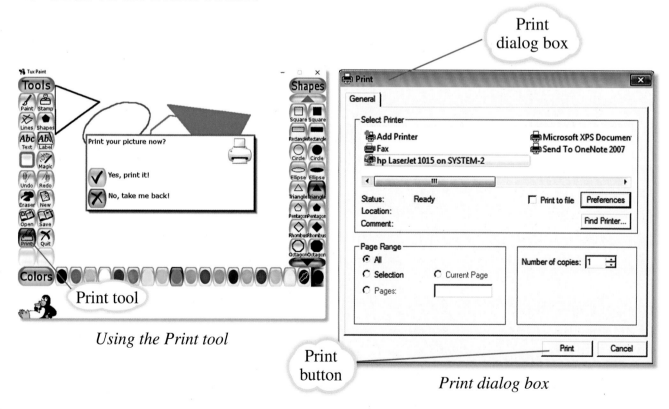

Using the Print tool

Print dialog box

Complete the following activity.

1. Create a storyboard using at least three canvasses in Tux Paint on the topic 'My Family Vacation'. Use different tools of Tux Paint to add interest to your pictures.

2. Set up a slide show in the class with the pictures running at a medium speed.

QUICK KEY

To open the list of saved pictures	Ctrl + O	To redo the last drawing action	Ctrl + R
To save a picture	Ctrl + S	To move to the next slide in the slide show	Enter / Space bar / Right Arrow key
To open a new Drawing Canvas	Ctrl + N	To move to the previous slide in the slide show	Left Arrow key
To undo the last drawing action	Ctrl + Z	To end the slide show	Esc key

GLOSSARY

Label   A tool which is used to type text in Tux Paint.

Stamp   A collection of readymade stickers and rubber stamps that can be put on pictures created in Tux Paint.

Slide show   A sequential movement of pictures on a computer.

1. Stamps can be put on pictures created in Tux Paint.

2. Stamps can be resized and reoriented depending on the requirement.

3. Different types of drawing canvasses are available to use in Tux Paint. A canvas may have a colored background, black-and-white drawing or a 3-D photograph.

4. A slide show can be set-up in Tux Paint. The sequence of slides and the speed of slide change can be specified.

5. The pictures created in Tux Paint can be printed using the Print tool.

6. The Label tool is used to write on any object or stamp.

EXERCISE

A. Solve the crossword using the clues given.

Across

2. Some .... can be flipped vertically.

4. The black-and-white outlines and 3-D pictures used as canvas in Tux Paint are called ....

5. It is a tool which is used to type text in Tux paint.

6. Pictures are saved as thumbnails in the virtual .... of Tux Paint.

Down

1. Tux Paint also has .... canvasses.

3. .... is a collection of rubber stamps and stickers.

4. It is the sequential movement of pictures on a computer.

B. **State the function of the following.**

1. Open
2.
3.
4. New

C. **True or false?**

1. A picture once selected for the slide show cannot be de-selected.
2. An outline of the stamp in the Drawing Canvas tells about its size and location.
3. The sequence of slides and the speed of slide change can not be specified.
4. 3-D photographs are available in Tux Paint for creating pictures.
5. Different tools available in Tux Paint cannot be used in one image.

D. **Which Tux tool/command is used to perform the activities given below?**

1. Display a cake for a birthday party. ....
2. Write 'Happy Birthday' on a balloon. ....
3. Print a hard copy of a drawing. ....
4. Display all the slides in a Picturebook. ....
5. Save a file with name 'Birthday Party'. ....

E. **Answer the following.**

1. Write the steps to print a picture in Tux Paint.
2. Write the steps to open a new Drawing Canvas in Tux Paint.
3. What are the different features of the Tux Paint Open tool?
4. What are the different ways in which a stamp can be modified?
5. Write the steps to create a slide show in Tux Paint.
6. What are the different types of drawing canvasses available in Tux Paint?
7. Name any two commonly used options present in the Print dialog box.

LAB WORK

A. Design a bed-sheet/curtain for your room using the Stamp tool. Use the additional features available with stamps, such as, flipping the stamp, creating its mirror image, etc. Save the file.

B. Create a virtual Picturebook using Tux Paint slides to display the scene of a zoo. You can use stamps to create it.

C. Use the Text tool in Tux Paint to create a slide show on five things you like to do during your summer break. Each slide should contain one point. Run the slide show in the class.

PROJECT WORK

Make a drawing in Tux Paint to depict the solar system. Show all planets in their orbits around the Sun and label them.

Polygons and Circles

Introduction

In this chapter, you will learn to draw different types of polygons. A polygon is the name for all closed figures with three or more sides like triangles, squares, pentagons and hexagons. You will learn to draw figures with a different number of edges. At the same time, you will learn how to move the turtle without drawing anything.

Drawing two lines with an angle

To make the turtle draw two lines with an angle, give the following set of instructions.

RT 180
FD 100
LT 90
FD 100

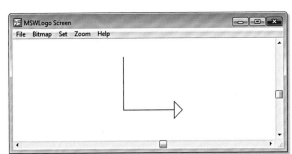

Two lines with an angle

Drawing a square

To draw a square, give the following instructions to the turtle. These instructions make the turtle 'walk' around the shape of a square.

FD 100

RT 90

FD 100

RT 90

FD 100

RT 90

FD 100

RT 90

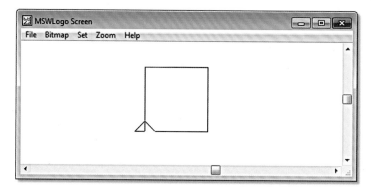

Square drawn by the turtle

Drawing a triangle

To make the turtle draw a triangle, give the following set of instructions.

FD 100	RT 120
RT 120	FD 100
FD 100	RT 120

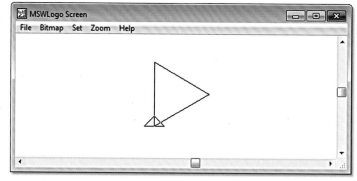

Triangle drawn by the turtle

PENUP (PU) command

PENUP (PU) command is used to lift the pen of the turtle from the screen. When this command is used, the turtle does not draw anything. You can move the turtle to any part of the screen without drawing anything.

FD 40	PU
RT 90	FD 40

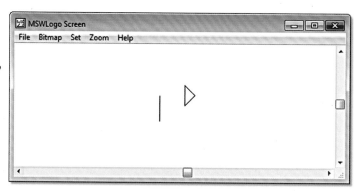

Using PENUP command

PENDOWN (PD) command

PENDOWN (PD) command puts the pen of the turtle down on the screen. The turtle will start drawing again when given the command.

FD 100	RT 90
RT 90	PD
PU	FD 100
FD 80	

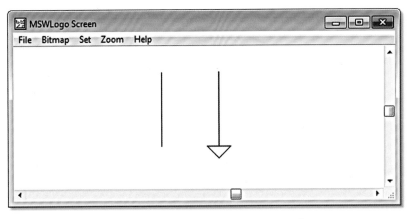

Using PENDOWN command

PENERASE (PE) command

PENERASE (PE) command drops the pen of the turtle and picks up the eraser. Any drawing command after PE command is used to erase the lines instead of drawing them.

FD 50
PE
BK 50

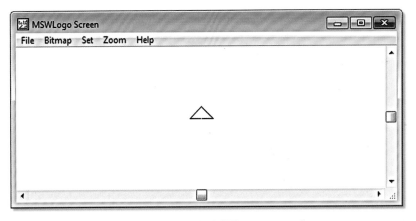

Using PENERASE command

PENNORMAL command

The PENNORMAL command makes the turtle behave normally. As you learnt, any command after using PE makes the turtle erase the drawing. To make it behave normally, use the PENNORMAL command. After this command, the turtle can draw anything.

HIDETURTLE (HT) command

The HT command hides the turtle. You can no longer see it on the screen. However, it will continue to follow the commands being given.

SHOWTURTLE (ST) command

The ST command displays the turtle when it is hidden by the HT command.

REPEAT command

This command repeats a list of instructions again and again for the specified number of times. REPEAT command is used to avoid repetitive work. When you have to draw figures like a square and a rectangle, you need to repeat the same set of commands. Use the REPEAT command to avoid this.

The REPEAT command requires two parameters: *the number of times to repeat* and *a list of commands to repeat.*

You need to give the following set of commands to draw a square in MSWLogo.

FD 100 RT 90   FD 100 RT 90
FD 100 RT 90   FD 100 RT 90

Drawing a square in MSWLogo

Here, the command FD 100 RT 90 is repeated four times. Instead of writing it again and again, you can use the REPEAT command as follows:
REPEAT 4 [FD 100 RT 90]

TRY THIS

REPEAT 12 [FD 100 RT 150]

What do you see after using this command?

Write MSWLogo commands to draw the following figures.

1.

2.

How to draw a circle

The REPEAT command is used to draw circles of different sizes. Some examples of the REPEAT command are given here.

Drawing a circle

Give the following command to tell the turtle to move one step forward and 1° to the right 360 times, to make a big circle.

REPEAT 360 [FD 1 RT 1]

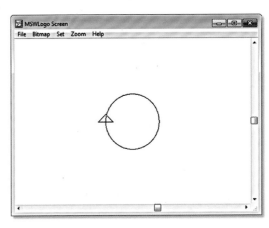

Drawing a big circle

TRY THIS

REPEAT 360 [FD 1 RT 1]
REPEAT 360 [FD 1 LT 1]
REPEAT 360 [FD 2 LT 1]
REPEAT 360 [FD 2 RT 1]

FACT FILE

The size of the circle reduces with the increase in the number of steps in FD command and the number of degrees in RT command, as the overall number of repetitions decrease.

Drawing a small circle

Give the following command to tell the turtle to move one step forward and 2° to the right 180 times, to make a smaller circle.

REPEAT 180 [FD 1 RT 2]

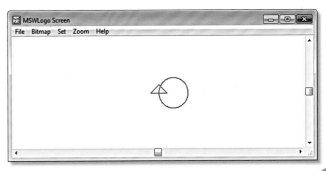

Drawing a small circle

TRY THIS

Find out what happens when you type the following command.

REPEAT 36 [RT 10 REPEAT 180 [FD 1 RT 2]]

ACTIVITY

Check the output of the following set of commands on the MSWLogo Screen.

HT REPEAT 360 [FD 1 RT 1]   REPEAT 180 [FD 1 RT 2]

REPEAT 90 [FD 1 RT 4]   REPEAT 45 [FD 1 RT 8]

How to draw an arc

Instead of rotating the turtle a full 360 degrees, if you turn it by fewer degrees, arcs of different sizes can be drawn. A few examples are given here.

TRY THIS

Run the commands and see what you get.

1. REPEAT 45 [FD 1 RT 1]
2. REPEAT 2 [REPEAT 180 [FD 1 RT 1]]

Drawing a semicircle

Give the following command to tell the turtle to move one step forward and 1° to the right 180 times to make a semicircle (arc). Then, to complete the semicircle, move it to the right by 90° and step forward 100 steps.

REPEAT 180 [FD 1 RT 1]
RT 90 FD 100

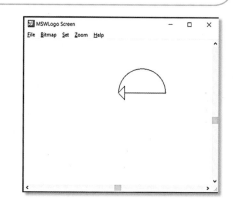

Drawing a semicircle

Drawing an arc

Give the following command to tell the turtle to move one step forward and 2° to the right 90 times to make an arc.

REPEAT 90 [FD 1 RT 2]

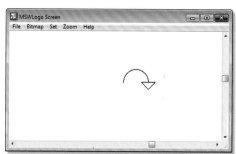

Drawing an arc

74

To make a closed figure with multiple sides use the formula:

REPEAT N [FD 50 RT D]

where N = Number of sides, D = 360/number of sides

For example, to make a pentagon, the command is: REPEAT 5 [FD 50 RT 72]

How to save an MSWLogo picture – BMP or GIF

The images created by the turtle can be saved for further use. The image can be saved in a BMP or GIF format.

Steps to save an MSWLogo picture

1. Select **Bitmap** menu ⟹ **Save/SaveAs** option.
2. A **Save As** dialog box opens. Type the file name and click on **Save**.

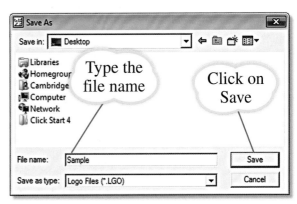

Save As dialog box

YOU ARE HERE

5

1. The PENUP or PU command is used to lift the pen of the turtle from the screen so that the turtle will not draw anything.

2. The PENDOWN or PD command puts the pen of the turtle down on the screen so that the turtle can start drawing again by giving commands.

3. The PENERASE or PE command drops the pen of the turtle and picks up the eraser.

4. The PENNORMAL command makes the turtle behave normally and stop working as an eraser.

5. The HIDETURTLE or HT command hides the turtle from the screen.

6. The SHOWTURTLE or ST command displays the turtle again when hidden using the HT command.

7. The REPEAT command repeats a list of instructions a specified number of times. This command is used to avoid repetitive work.

A. Fill in the blanks.

1. A .... is the name for all closed figures with a certain number of edges.
2. The .... command is used to lift the pen of the turtle from the screen.
3. The .... command hides the turtle.
4. The REPEAT command requires two parameters: the number of times to repeat and a .... to repeat.

B. True or false?

1. The PU command puts the pen of the turtle down on the screen.

2. The PE command drops the pen of the turtle and picks up the eraser.

3. The PENDOWN command makes the turtle behave normally.

4. The HT command displays the turtle when it is hidden after using the ST command.

5. The REPEAT command is used to save repetitive work.

C. Give commands to do the following work.

1. Draw the shape of a half-moon.
2. Draw a cone.
3. Draw a dotted rhombus 50 long.
4. Draw a flower using the REPEAT command.

D. Draw the output for the following commands.

1. FD 50   LT 90
   LT 90   FD 20
   FD 30   LT 90
   RT 90   FD 30
   BK 40

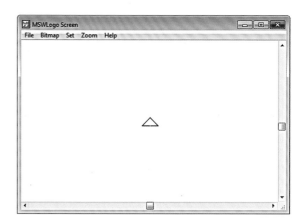

2.

FD 60	PU
BK 120	RT 90
FD 60	FD 50
RT 90	LT 90
FD 50	PD
LT 90	FD 60
FD 60	BK 120
BK 120	FD 120
FD 60	

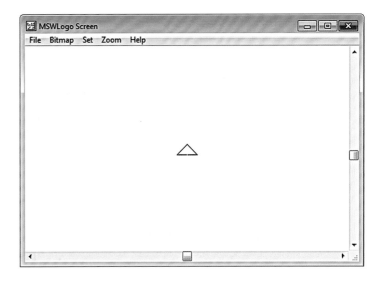

E. Answer the following questions.

1. Why do you use the HIDETURTLE and SHOWTURTLE commands?
2. Write the instructions to draw a triangle, with a length of 50 for each side, using the REPEAT command.
3. What is the use of the PENNORMAL command?
4. State the difference between the PENUP and PENDOWN commands.

LAB WORK

A. Write down the commands to draw the following figures.

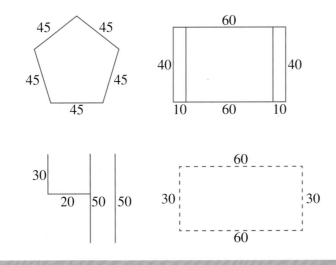

B. Open the MSWLogo Screen and see the output of the following commands.

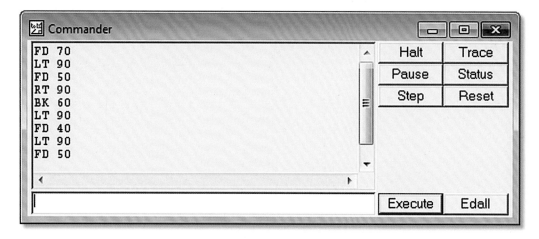

PROJECT WORK

Work in groups of four. Each group will write a command to make any 4 capital letters of the alphabet and a picture of a favourite toy, using lines, circles or polygons.

Submit the project in a Word file by pasting the drawings along with the commands required to create them.

MSWLogo – Using PenColors and PenSizes

SNAP RECAP

1. Which command drops the pen of the turtle and picks up the eraser?
2. Which command is used to avoid repetitive work?
3. Which command hides the turtle on the screen?
4. Write the command to draw a circle.

LEARNING OBJECTIVES

You will learn about:
- SETPENSIZE and SETPENCOLOR commands
- coloring an object using SETFLOODCOLOR and FILL commands
- SETSCREENCOLOR command
- checking the status of the turtle

Introduction

You can change the size and color of the pen of the turtle in MSWLogo. This is done using the SETPENSIZE and SETPENCOLOR commands respectively.

SETPENSIZE command

The SETPENSIZE command changes the height and width of the pen of the turtle.

SETPENSIZE [NUM1 NUM2]

Here NUM1 is the height and NUM2 is the width.

Height: The height has an insignificant effect on the pen. The height can be overruled by the FD or BK commands.

Width: The thickness of the pen can be changed in **pixels** by using a numeric value.

Pixels are the smallest picture elements.

To get the output shown in the screenshot on the right, you need to follow the set of commands given below.

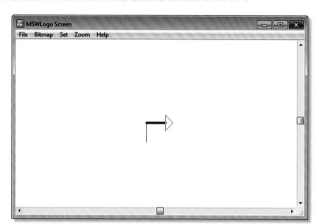

FD 40
SETPENSIZE [5 5]
RT 90
FD 40

Here the size of the pen is 5 pixels in thickness with an insignificant effect of length 5.

The two numeric values given with the SETPENSIZE command are generally kept the same. However, MSWLogo uses the value for the width only.

Changing pen size using the menu bar

You can change the size of the pen using the Menu bar. You need to follow the steps given below.

1. Click on the **Set** tab ⟹ **PenSize...** option.
2. The **Pen Size** dialog box opens. Select the pen size you want then click on **OK**.

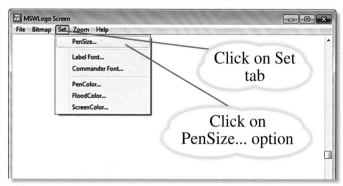

Changing the pen size using the Menu bar

Pen Size dialog box

SETPENCOLOR command

This command is used to change the pen color of the turtle. MSWLogo uses the three primary colors – red, blue and green – in different combinations. These combinations make a variety of colors for the pen. Each of these three colors has a number range of 0 to 255. By varying these numbers for all three colors you can create 16.7 million different colours!

Some of the combinations are already made for you. These are:

SETPENCOLOR [000 000 000]	Black
SETPENCOLOR [255 255 255]	White
SETPENCOLOR [128 128 128]	Grey
SETPENCOLOR [255 000 000]	Red
SETPENCOLOR [000 255 000]	Green
SETPENCOLOR [000 000 255]	Blue

To get the output shown in the picture on the right, you need to follow the commands given below.

FD 50
SETPENCOLOR
[000 255 000]
SETPENSIZE [4 4]
RT 90
FD 40

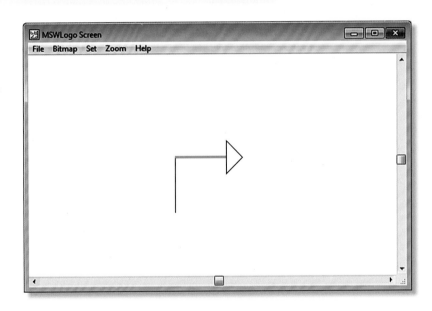

Changing the pen color using the Menu bar

You can change the pen color using the Menu bar. Follow the steps given below.

1. Click on the **Set tab** ⟹ **PenColor...** option.
2. The **Pen Color** dialog box appears. Select the color you want then click on **OK**.

Pen Color dialog box

ACTIVITY

Complete the following activity.

1. Create a red equilateral triangle with a thick border to look like a clown's hat.

2. Below the triangle, create a circle with a thick yellow border to look like the clown's face.

Coloring an object

Any figure can be filled with color in MSWLogo.

Steps to fill color in a figure

1. Set the color of the brush using the **SETFLOODCOLOR** command.

2. Fill the chosen color in an enclosed figure using the **FILL** command.

SETFLOODCOLOR command

The SETFLOODCOLOR command sets the color of the brush. The pen of the turtle acts as a brush using this command. All the three primary colors with values ranging from 0 to 255 are used together to make different colors.

For example, to set the color blue, you need to give the following command:

SETFLOODCOLOR [0 0 255]

Steps to set FLOODCOLOR using the Menu bar

You can do the same by using the Menu bar.

1. Click on **Set** tab ⟹ **FloodColor...** option.
2. A **Flood Color** dialog box opens (Fig. 6.6). Select the color then click on **OK**.

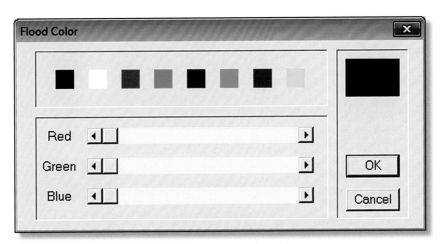

Flood Color dialog box

FILL command

The FILL command uses the color of the brush, set by using SETFLOODCOLOR, to flood an area. Both the commands have to work together to give a colorful object.

To fill blue color in the given figure, you need to give the following commands.

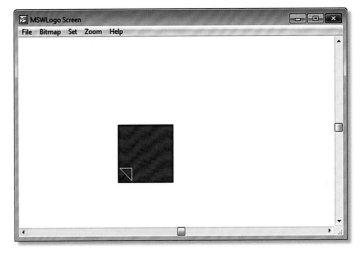

To fill blue color in a square

REPEAT 4 [FD 100 RT 90]
RT 45
FD 20

SETFLOODCOLOR [0 0 255]
FILL

The color will fill a closed figure when the turtle is inside the figure.

To create a colored boundary/border for a figure, you need to give the following commands.

REPEAT 4 [FD 50 RT 90]: Creates a square with sides 50.

PU: PENUP

RT 35: Sets the direction of the turtle at 35°.

SETFLOODCOLOR [0 255 0]: Sets the color to be flooded where the turtle is placed.

FILL: Effects of the SETFLOODCOLOR command can be seen.

SETSCREENCOLOR command

The SETSCREENCOLOR command sets the background color of the screen. You can use the three primary colors in varied combinations to obtain different colors.

You need to give the following set of commands to create a colored border triangle on a blue background.

SETSCREENCOLOR [0 0 255]   SETPENCOLOR [255 0 0]

SETPENSIZE [2 10]   REPEAT 3[FD 100 RT 120]

Colored triangle on a blue background

TRY THIS

Try these commands to flood the entire screen with blue color.

SETFLOODCOLOR [0 0 255]   FILL

84

Complete the activity given on page 82 as below.

1. Fill the clown's hat with red color.

2. Fill the clown's face with yellow color.

3. Change the background color of the screen to blue.

Checking the status of the Turtle

You might forget about the status of the turtle after giving several commands. Status refers to the position of the pen, the position of the turtle on the screen, the color of the background, etc. All this can be checked by giving the following commands.

STATUS command

The STATUS command opens a Status window. It tells you the current settings of the turtle.

Status	
Pen	
Contact:	Down
Width:	10
Style:	Normal
Orientation	
Heading:	0.00
Pitch:	0.00
Roll:	0.00
Turtle	
Position(XYZ):	0,0,0
Which:	0
Visibility:	Shown
Color	
Pen(RGB):	255,0,0
Flood(RGB):	0,0,0
Screen(RGB):	0,0,255
Palette use:	N/A
Kernel	
Calls:	7
Peak Memory:	6000 Nodes
Vectors:	3

Shows the pen setting

Shows the position of turtle

Shows the color settings

Status window

NOSTATUS command

The Status window can be removed from the screen by giving the NOSTATUS command.

Check the status of the turtle by clicking on the **Status** button in the Commander Window. As soon as you click on it, the **Status** dialog box appears showing the exact status of the turtle. The Commander Window now shows the **NoStatus** option that closes the Status dialog box when clicked.

GLOSSARY

FILL command   Uses color of the brush to flood an area.

NOSTATUS command   Removes the Status window from the screen.

Pixels   These are the smallest picture elements.

SETFLOODCOLOR command   Sets the color of the brush.

SETPENCOLOR command   Gives ink color to the pen of the turtle.

SETPENSIZE command   Changes the size of the pen of the turtle.

SETSCREENCOLOR command   Sets the color of the background screen.

STATUS command   Displays the status of the turtle.

YOU ARE HERE

6

1. You can change the height and width of the pen of the turtle.
2. MSWLogo uses the three primary colors – red, blue and green – in different combinations. These combinations give different colors to the pen.
3. The pen of the turtle acts as a brush using the SETFLOODCOLOR command.
4. The SETSCREENCOLOR command uses the three primary colors in varied combinations to give different colors to the background screen.

EXERCISE

A.   Fill in the blanks.

1. The .... command changes the size of the pen of the turtle.
2. The .... of the pen can be changed in pixels by using a numeric value.
3. .... are the smallest picture elements.
4. The .... command is used to give the ink color to the pen of the turtle.
5. The .... command sets the color of the brush.

B. True or false?

1. The SETBACKGROUNDCOLOR command sets the color of the background of the screen.

2. To add color to an object, it is not necessary to use the FILL command and SETFLOODCOLOR together.

3. The STATUS command removes the Status window from the screen.

4. The colors range from 0 to 255.

5. Red, blue and green are secondary colors.

C. Answer the following questions.

1. How can you change the pen color using the Menu bar?

2. How do you change the size of the pen of the turtle?

3. Give commands to create a colored boundary/border to a given figure.

4. What is the purpose of the SETPENSIZE command?

5. How can you show and hide the status of the turtle?

6. Can you fill a square with color by using the following commands in MSWLogo? Give reasons.

   a. FD 100 RT 90 FD 100 RT 90 FD 100 RT 90 FD 10 RT 90 SETFLOODCOLOR [0 255 0] FILL

   b. FD 100 RT 90 FD 100 RT 90 FD 100 RT 90 FD 10 RT 90 SETSCREENCOLOR [0 255 0] FILL

D. State the difference between the following.

1. SETPENCOLOR and SETPENSIZE commands

2. SETFLOODCOLOR and SETSCREENCOLOR commands

3. STATUS and NOSTATUS commands

A. Make the following figures in MSWLogo.

 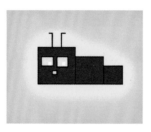  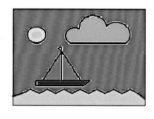

B. Open the MSWLogo screen and find out the output on typing the following commands.

1. FD 50
   SETPENSIZE [6 6]
   RT 90
   FD 60

2. FD 50
   SETPENCOLOR
   [000 255 000]
   SETPENSIZE [6 6]
   RT 90
   FD 60

   SETPENCOLOR
   [000 000 255]
   SETPENSIZE [4 4]
   RT 90
   FD 60

PROJECT WORK

Make a big circle with 9 smaller and smaller circles inside each other that share the same centre point using MSWLogo commands. Using SETFLOODCOLOR, make ten new colors and fill each circle with these new colors.

WHO AM I?

I was born on February 29, 1928 in Pretoria, South Africa.

I am a well-known mathematician, computer scientist and an educator. I am the inventor of the Logo programming language.

I am ....

MSWLogo – Text Commands and Arithmetic Operations

SNAP RECAP

1. How can you check the status of the Turtle?
2. Discuss the purpose of the FILL, SETSCREENCOLOR and SETPENSIZE commands.

LEARNING OBJECTIVES

You will learn about:
- MAKE, SHOW, PRINT, LABEL and TYPE commands
- arithmetic operators like +, -, *, /
- operator commands like SUM, DIFFERENCE, PRODUCT, QUOTIENT and REMAINDER

Introduction

In MSWLogo, you can work with text using the turtle. All the commands that are given in this chapter are used with text data. You can also perform arithmetic operations in MSWLogo. The mathematical work done with numbers is called an **arithmetic operation**. For example, addition, subtraction, etc. are arithmetic operations.

In this chapter, you will learn to handle different numbers in MSWLogo. You can also perform arithmetic operations on them by using different arithmetic symbols. In MSWLogo, there are two ways to perform these calculations. Firstly, by using the arithmetic operators and secondly, by using the operator commands.

MAKE command

The MAKE command is used to assign a value to a **variable**.

Variable

A variable is a memory container which holds a value. The value of this container may vary depending on the user. A value assigned to it can be changed anytime. For example,

If A = 2, then 5 + A = 7.

Here 'A' is a variable that holds the value 2. But the value of 'A' can be changed by redefining the variable.

To define a variable, you need to learn about the variablename and value.

Variablename: The name of the variable to which you wish to assign a value. Basic rules to define variablename are:

1. Variablename must start with a letter.
2. Spaces in variablename are not allowed.

Value: The thing to be assigned to a variable. This can be a number or text.

Therefore, you write: MAKE "Variablename Value

The variablename value is preceded by an opening double quote (").

For example, to create a variable named Num with value 5, you need to give the following command.
MAKE "NUM 5

To create a variable named WELCOME with text value 'Hello WELCOME to Lab', you need to give the following command.
MAKE "WELCOME [Hello WELCOME to Lab]

You can create three variables A, B and C with values 5, 6 and 10, respectively. To do so, give the following set of commands.
MAKE "A 5   MAKE "B 6   MAKE "C 10

SHOW command

The SHOW command is used to display the value of the variable created using the MAKE command.

To display the value assigned to a variable it should be preceded by a colon (:). Remember to leave a single space between the SHOW command and the colon.

For example, to display the value of the variable created using the command given below:

MAKE "NUM 5
You need to give the following command:

SHOW :NUM
It displays the value 5.

To display the value of the variable created using the command given below:

MAKE "WELCOME [Hello]
You need to give the following command:

SHOW :WELCOME

It displays [Hello]

You can display values of different variables by using a single SHOW command.

For example, you can display the values of the commands MAKE "NUM 5 and MAKE "WELCOME [Hello] by using a single SHOW command as shown in the screenshot on the right.

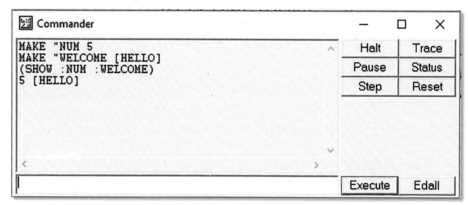

Commander Window with SHOW command

(SHOW :NUM :WELCOME)

It displays 5 [Hello]

PRINT command

The PRINT command is used to give the output in the Commander window. This output can be in the form of a variable name to display the assigned value. For example, to print 5 and 6 on the monitor, the following commands are used.

MAKE "N1 5

MAKE "N2 6

PRINT :N1

5

(PRINT :N1 :N2)

5 6

Commander Window with PRINT command

The output can also be in the form of text. The text is displayed as it is. For example to print the messages 'Hello' and 'Hello World', the commands are given here.

PRINT "Hello

Hello

PRINT [HELLO WORLD]

HELLO WORLD

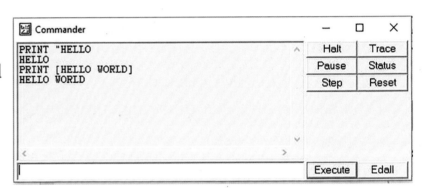

Commander Window to display Hello World

If the text is more than one word, then square brackets are needed.

TRY THIS

Use PR instead of PRINT to display anything.

LABEL command

The LABEL command displays the output on the MSWLogo screen. This output can be one word or a collection of words as well as any text or number(s).

This text will be printed at the current angle and position of the turtle. The angle of the text can be controlled by using the RT and LT commands. The color of the text can be controlled by using the SETPENCOLOR command.

For example, to display the message 'HI I AM ENJOYING LOGO' on the MSWLogo screen, give the commands shown in the screenshot.

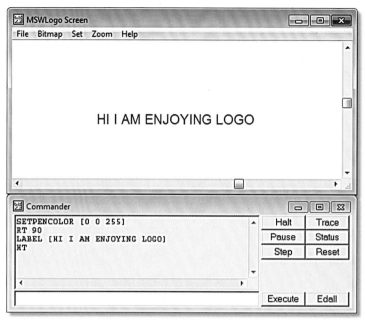

Using LABEL command

ACTIVITY

A. What will be the output of the following set of commands?

1. SETPENCOLOR [0 0 255] RT 45 LABEL [******]

2. SETPENCOLOR [255 0 255] REPEAT 12 [RT 45 LABEL [******]

3. SETPENCOLOR [255 255 0] REPEAT 12 [RT 120 LABEL [########]

Create a few more commands like this and see their results in MSWLogo.

B. Write the commands to create the following pattern.

  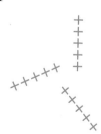

(Hint: Use the PU and HT commands.)

TYPE command

The TYPE command is used to print the output to the buffer. It means that the text with the TYPE command will not be printed in the Commander Window unless you use either the PRINT or SHOW command. For example, give the following set of commands:

TYPE "hello

PRINT "hi

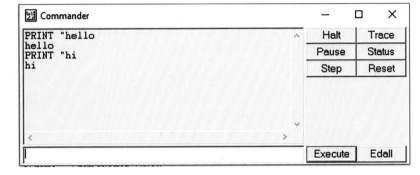

Using the TYPE command

Buffering makes the program much faster than it would be if each character appeared immediately.

Arithmetic Operations in MSWLogo

There are four arithmetic operators. These are in the table below.

Arithmetic operators

Operator	Meaning	Operator	Meaning
+	Addition	*	Multiplication
–	Subtraction	/	Division

The results of the calculations done using arithmetic operators are seen in the Recall List box of the Commander window if given independently.

FACT FILE

The numbers on the left and the right side of the operator are known as operands.

To print the sum of two numbers, say 2 and 35, the command is:

PRINT 2 + 35

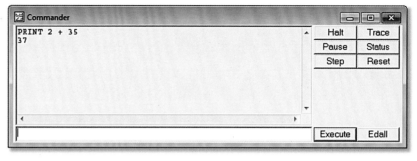

Using + operator

To print the difference of two numbers, say 12 and 3, the command is

PRINT 12 – 3

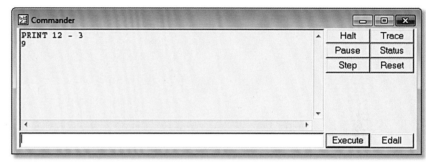

Using – operator

To multiply two numbers, say 10 and 220, the command is:

PRINT 10 * 220

The arithmetic operator used for multiplication is * and not **x** as you do in mathematics.

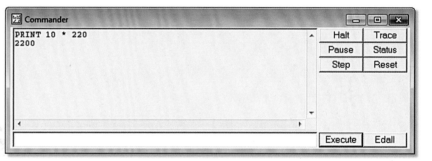

*Using * operator*

To divide two numbers, say 10 and 5, the command is:

PRINT 10 / 5

The first number is divided by the second number.

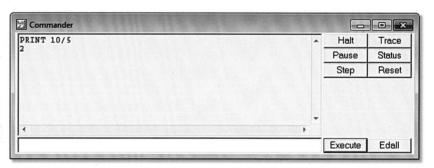

Using / operator

Arithmetic operations using operator commands

In MSWLogo, arithmetic operations can also be done by using operator commands. These are given in the table below. Results of these commands are also seen in the Commander window.

Arithmetic operators

Operator command	Usage
SUM	Used for addition
DIFFERENCE	Used for subtraction
PRODUCT	Used for multiplication
QUOTIENT	Used for division where the answer is the first number divided by the second number
REMAINDER	Used for division where the answer is the remainder value

SUM

The SUM command is used to add two or more numbers. For example, to print the sum of two numbers, say 2 and 3, the command is:
PRINT SUM 2 3

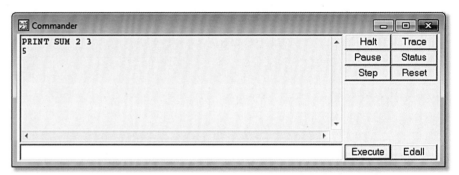

Using the SUM command for addition of two numbers

To print the sum of more than two numbers, say 2, 3, 4 and 5, the command is:
PRINT (SUM 2 3 4 5)

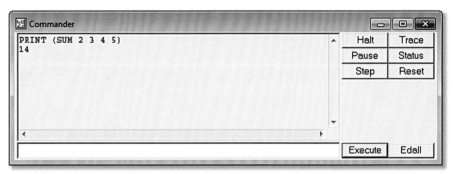

Using the SUM command for addition of more than two numbers

Curve brackets are compulsory if more than two numbers are used for addition.

DIFFERENCE

The DIFFERENCE command is used to give the difference between two numbers. For example, to print the difference of two numbers, the command is:

PRINT DIFFERENCE 7 2

PRINT DIFFERENCE 7 10

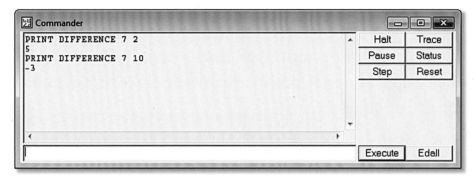

Using the DIFFERENCE command

PRODUCT

The PRODUCT command is used for multiplication of two or more numbers. For example, to print the product of two or more numbers, the command is:

PRINT PRODUCT 5 2

PRINT (PRODUCT 11 2 2)

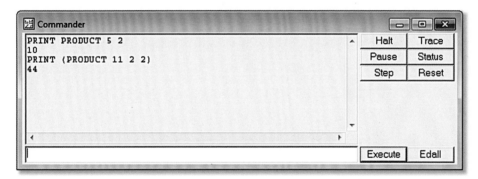

Using PRODUCT command

QUOTIENT

The QUOTIENT command divides two numbers, and gives the answer. If only one number is specified by the user, then it assumes the first number to be 1. The number given by the user is taken as the second number. It divides the first number by the second and gives the answer.

For example, to divide two numbers, the command is:

PRINT QUOTIENT 4 2

PRINT (QUOTIENT 4)

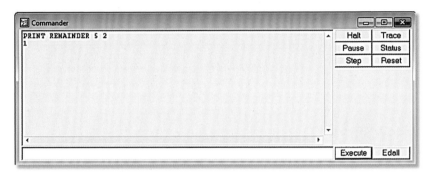

Using the QUOTIENT command

REMAINDER

The REMAINDER operator command displays only the remainder of the division as the result. The first number is divided by the second number and the remainder is displayed.

For example, MSWLogo will print 1 as the result on the screen for the command:

PRINT REMAINDER 5 2

Using REMAINDER command

TRY THIS

MSWLogo has GREATER THAN (>) and LESS THAN (<) commands that can be used to compare two numbers. If the comparison is correct, MSWLogo will show 'true' as the answer or vice versa. Now, check PR 48>69 and PR 68<97.

ACTIVITY

Print the result of the following arithmetic operations in MSWLogo.

1. 50 – 22 + 10 * 2

2. 1000 / 3 * 2 + 70

GLOSSARY

Arithmetic operation   The mathematical work done on numbers.

LABEL command   Displays the output on the MSWLogo Screen.

MAKE command   Used to assign a value to a variable.

PRINT command   Used to write anything on the Commander Window.

SHOW command   Displays value of the variable created using MAKE command.

TYPE command   Used to print the output to the buffer.

Value   The thing to be assigned to a variable.

Variable   A memory container which holds a value.

Variable name   Any name of the variable that you wish to assign.

YOU ARE HERE

7

1. The turtle of the MSWLogo can be used to display text along with figures which it can draw easily.

2. The various commands used in MSWLogo to handle data include MAKE, SHOW, PRINT, LABEL and TYPE.

3. MSWLogo can handle numbers well. All the arithmetic operations can be performed on numbers.

4. Arithmetic operations in MSWLogo can be done using arithmetic operators like +, -, *, /.

5. Arithmetic operations can also be performed by using operator commands.

6. The various operator commands are SUM for addition, DIFFERENCE for subtraction, PRODUCT for multiplication, QUOTIENT for dividing and REMAINDER for giving the remainder of a division.

EXERCISE

A. **Fill in the blanks with the correct word.**

> Numbers   LABEL   Remainder   Buffer   Variable

1. The TYPE command prints the output to the ....
2. A .... is a memory container which holds a value.
3. The .... command is used to display the output on the MSWLogo Screen.
4. Arithmetic operators work on ....
5. The REMAINDER command gives you the .... of the division of two numbers.

B. **Name the following commands.**

1. This command is used to write anything in the Commander window. ....
2. This command is used to print the output to the buffer. ....
3. This command is used to assign a text value to a variable. ....
4. This command is used to display the output on the MSWLogo Screen. ....
5. This command is used to display the value of the variable created using the MAKE command. ....

C. **State the differences between the following commands:**

1. PRINT and TYPE
2. MAKE and SHOW
3. PRINT and LABEL
4. QUOTIENT and REMAINDER

D. **Spot the error(s) in the following commands.**

1. MAKE "NAME "AJAY
   MAKE "AGE 10
   SHOW :NAME :AGE
2. TYPE "SAVE TIGERS
   PRINT"
3. REMAINDER PRINT 15 6
4. 2 + 3 PRINT
5. PRIN 15/4

E. **Give the MSWLogo commands for the following:**

1. to find out the addition of 10 and 12.
2. to calculate the remainder when 26 is divided by 3.

3. to calculate the difference between 34 and 4.

4. to multiply 12 by 3.

F. Answer the following questions.

1. What is the purpose of the MAKE command?

2. What is the importance of the TYPE command?

3. What is a variable? Give two examples of a variable.

4. Can you do addition in MSWLogo without using the SUM command? If yes, then how?

5. Catherine forgot how to use the PRODUCT command to multiply two numbers. Suggest an alternative method in MSWLogo to achieve the result.

LAB WORK

A. Open the MSWLogo Screen and see the output for the following commands.

1. PRINT [My Name is ……………]; type your name here

2. Type [My Name is ……]

    Print "…………; type your name here

B. Practise the MSWLogo operator commands. Write the commands to get the output of the following statements:

1. $4 \div 2 \times 8 + 3 - 2$

2. Display the 'quotient' when 25 is divided by 7

3. Display the 'remainder' when 36 is divided by 5

C. Create a formula to calculate the area and the perimeter of a rectangle. Find out the answer using MSWLogo commands, if length = 3 units and breadth = 4 units.

PROJECT WORK

Write the MSWLogo commands to assign a student's marks for five subjects using five different variables. Find and print the total marks out of 500. Then, calculate the percentage.

Introduction to MS PowerPoint 2010

LEARNING OBJECTIVES

You will learn about:
- starting MS PowerPoint 2010
- the MS PowerPoint 2010 window
- creating and saving a new presentation
- slide layouts

- MS PowerPoint 2010 views
- running a slide show
- opening an existing presentation
- printing a presentation
- closing and exiting MS PowerPoint 2010

Introduction

MS PowerPoint is a software program used to create presentations. It is a powerful tool for communicating ideas and information. It can include text, graphics, pictures, movies, sounds, special effects, etc.

A MS PowerPoint Presentation consists of **slides**. These slides are organised and formatted using various features of MS PowerPoint. It is a way of presenting your viewpoint in the form of text and graphics on the slides. These slides are just like the pages of a document. It can contain either text or graphics, or both. It runs continuously as a **slide show**. This chapter will discuss using MS PowerPoint 2010. For MS PowerPoint 2016 updates, go to the end of the chapter.

Starting MS PowerPoint 2010

Follow these steps to start MS PowerPoint 2010.

1. Click on **Start** ⟹ **All Programs** ⟹ **Microsoft Office** ⟹ **Microsoft PowerPoint 2010**.

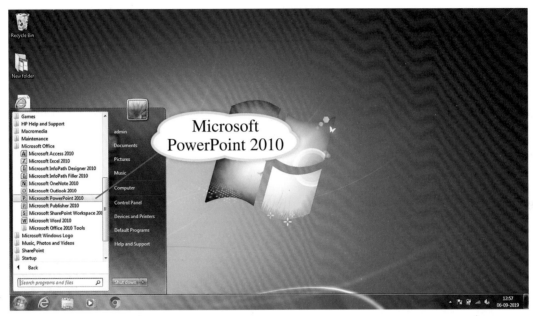

Starting MS PowerPoint 2010

2. The MS PowerPoint 2010 window appears.

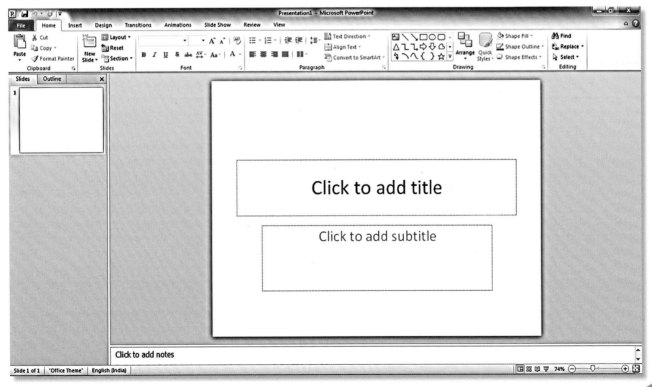

The MS PowerPoint 2010 window

Double-click on the Microsoft PowerPoint 2010 icon on the desktop to open the PowerPoint 2010 window.

Components of the MS PowerPoint 2010 window

The PowerPoint window displays information about a presentation. It includes tools to create and edit presentations.

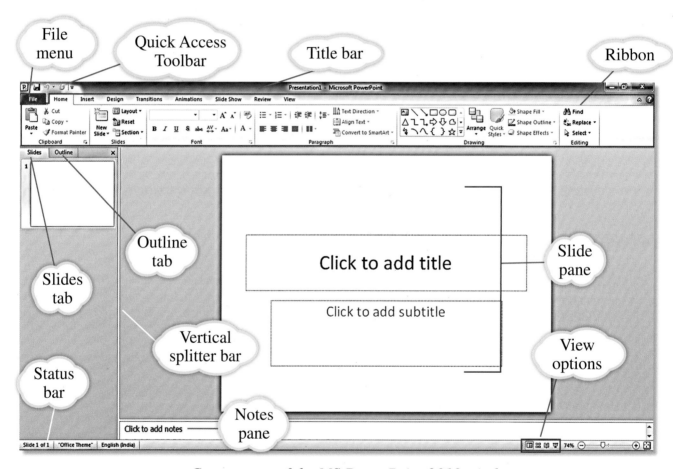

Components of the MS PowerPoint 2010 window

The different components of MS PowerPoint 2010 are explained in the table below.

Components	Definition
Title bar	Displays the name of the software application and the name of the file currently in use. It has Minimize, Maximize and Close options. Presentation1 is the default name of a presentation.
File menu	Appears in the upper-left corner of the window and contains options like New, Open, Save, Save As and Print.
Ribbon	Appears below the Title bar. It is divided into tabs which are further divided into groups. Each group has a number of options.
Quick Access Toolbar	Contains some of the most commonly used options like Undo, Redo and Save. More options can be added to it from the Ribbon.
Slides tab	Displays the slides of the presentation as miniatures called **thumbnails**. You can move to any slide in the presentation by clicking on this tab.
Outline tab	Displays the slide text.
Slide pane	On the right side of the PowerPoint window where the current slide can be edited. It is separated from the left pane by the **Vertical splitter bar**. It can be resized by dragging its top or right border.
Status bar	Appears at the bottom of the window. It displays the serial number of the slide, total number of slides, default language, etc.
Notes pane	Displays the notes created by the speaker for the content in the slide pane. It appears below the slide pane.
View options	Helps to switch between different views. These views are Normal, Slide Sorter and Slide Show. The default view is Normal where the window is divided into three panes.

Creating a new presentation

1. Click on the **File** menu.

2. Select the **New** option from the drop-down list.

3. The **New Presentation** dialog box appears. Select **Blank presentation** option from the **Available Templates and Themes** option and click on **Create** button.

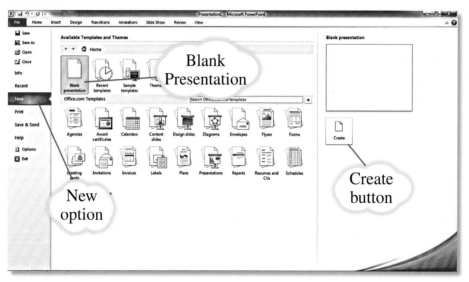

Creating a new presentation

4. A new presentation opens with the Title Slide.

5. To add a new slide with a different layout, click on the **New Slide** drop-down list in the **Slides** group of the **Home** tab and select your chosen slide layout.

To add another slide with the same layout as the current slide, select the **Duplicate Selected Slides** option in the **New Slide** drop-down list.

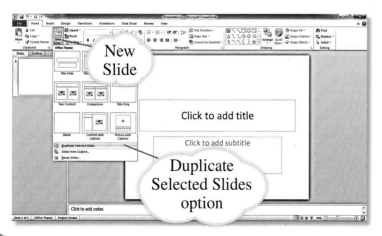

Inserting a new slide

FACT FILE

You may add clip arts, pictures or charts to your slides. You may even add music to your presentation.

Saving a presentation

1. Click on the **File** menu and select **Save/Save As** option from the drop-down list.

2. The **Save As** dialog box appears. Select the destination folder from the options given in the left pane and type the file name. Click on the **Save** button.

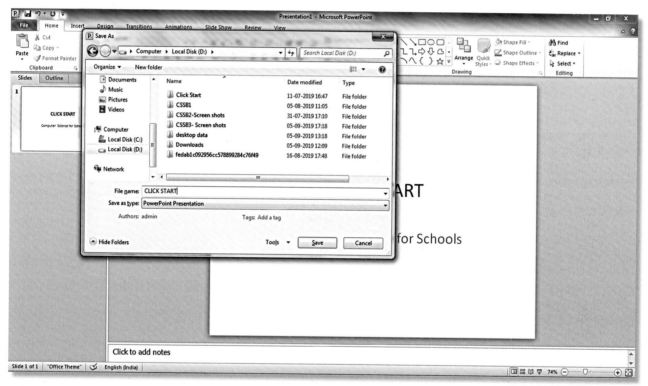

Saving a presentation

MS PowerPoint 2010 saves a file with the extension .pptx by default. Any changes made to the saved presentation can be saved directly by clicking the **Save** option in the **File Menu** drop-down list or in the **Quick Access Toolbar**.

TRY THIS

Save your file in PowerPoint 97-2007 Presentation format and find out the file extension.

Slide layout

The slide layout is the arrangement of text and graphics on the slide. The title slide usually includes the title and the subtitle. To select slide layouts, click on the **Layout** drop-down list in the **Slides** group of the **Home** tab.

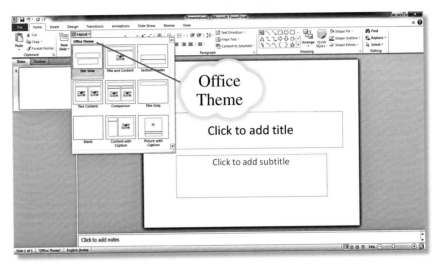

Slide layouts in MS PowerPoint 2010

The **Office Theme** section in the drop-down list is used to select different templates for the different slides.

Some of the slide layouts available in PowerPoint are shown in the screenshot above.

You will notice in the **Office Theme** section, that the first slide is the **Title Slide** of a presentation. In MS PowerPoint 2010, the **Title Slide** always appears first by default.

Worked example

You will now create a presentation on how to make a great Tricolor Sandwich. Open up PowerPoint to get started!

Slide 1

You will notice in the lower-left corner of the screen, Slide 1 of 1 is indicated.

1. Place your cursor on the 'Click to add title' box. You will see a blinking cursor, after clicking in the box.

2. To insert the text in this formatted text box, simply enter (type-in) the title:

   HOW TO MAKE A GREAT TRICOLOR SANDWICH

3. Now, click on the second box 'Click to add subtitle' and type:

> FIRELESS COOKING (Press the **Enter** key.)
>
> by (Press the **Enter** key.)
>
> Your Name (Type in your name.)

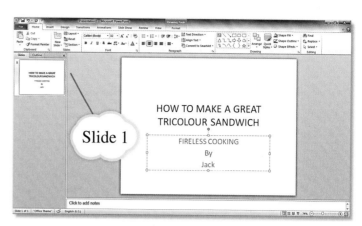

Subtitle box

After you type in both the boxes, your Slide 1 will look like the one in the picture above.

Slide 2

Now move on to the next slide. At the top of the screen, in the **Slides** group of the **Home** tab you will see a **New Slide** option. Click on it. A new slide appears in the centre section of the screen. Use the **New Slide** drop-down list to choose a different template from the **Office Theme** section. Select the template displayed below.

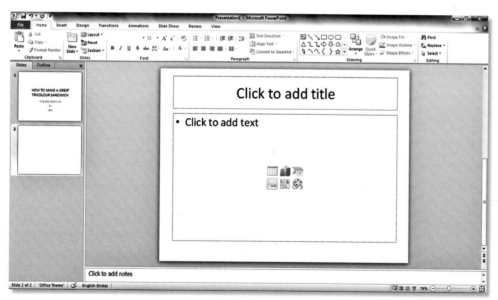

Selected slide

1. Click on the 'Click to add title' box and type: INGREDIENTS.
2. Click on the 'Click to add text' box and type:

> Three slices of white bread (Press **Enter** key.)
>
> Homemade orange jam (Press **Enter** key.)

One slice of cheese (Press **Enter** key.)

Notice how each line appears with a 'bullet' (•) before it.

Keep on adding the slides of your choice in the presentation.

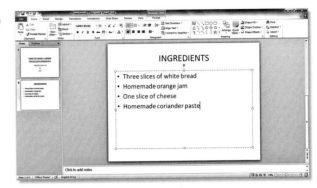

Slide 2

MS PowerPoint 2010 Views

MS PowerPoint 2010 can be seen using different views.

Normal View

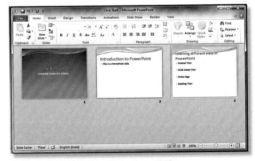

Slide Sorter View

Notes Page

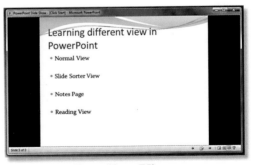

Reading View

MS PowerPoint 2010 Views

Normal View

Normal view displays the current slide in the Slide pane. It is best for editing the text and graphics on a slide. The left pane can be used to display slides. Click on a slide in the Slides tab or click on a slide icon in the Outline tab to display the slide in the Slide pane. Slide order is changed in Normal view by dragging slide icons in the Outline tab or in the Slides tab.

Slide Sorter View

Slide Sorter view is useful for selecting multiple slides. It is also useful for changing the order of slides. Drag a slide to another position to change the order of the presentation.

Notes Page

This view displays one slide at a time with an area below to add extra notes about the content. These notes work as a reference for the presenter.

Reading View

This is a new view in PowerPoint 2010. It allows you to view the presentation as a slideshow with complete access to the application window. No changes are allowed in this view but it gives a preview of the complete presentation.

Slide Show

Slide Show displays the presentation as it will appear to the audience. It starts with slide 1 regardless of which slide is currently being displayed. Click **Esc** key to end the slide show.

QUICK KEY

The previous slide	**Page Up**
The next slide	**Page Down**
The first slide	**Ctrl + Home**
The last slide	**Ctrl + End**

Running a Slide Show

Once your presentation is ready, then start the slide show as follows:

Click on **View** tab ⟹ **Presentation Views** group ⟹ **Slide Show** option.

Click on **Slide Show** tab ⟹ **Start Slide Show** group ⟹ **From Beginning** option.

Press **F5**.

The slides are displayed in full-screen size and the PowerPoint window is no longer visible. During a slide show a toolbar at the lower-left corner of the screen is displayed. You can select an option to display the previous or next slide, or display a menu of options.

Navigate through the presentation in a slide show

1. To display the next slide, click the left mouse button or press the **N** key, the **Page down** key, or the **Space bar** key.
2. To display the previous slide, press the **P** key, the **Page up** key, or the **Backspace** key.
3. To re-display the hidden pointer and/or change the pointer to a pen, press **Ctrl + P** keys.
4. To re-display the hidden pointer and/or change the pointer to an arrow, press **Ctrl + A** keys.
5. To end the slide show, press the **Esc** key.

Complete the following activity.

1. Open your presentation MySchool.pptx in the Slide Sorter View and see the difference.

2. Change the order of a few slides by dragging them either to the right or to the left.

3. Go to View ⟹ Presentation Views ⟹ Slide Show option to run your presentation.

Opening an existing presentation

To open an existing presentation follow the steps below.

1. Click on the **File** menu.

2. Select the **Open** option from the drop-down list.

3. The **Open** dialog box appears.

Specify a name and location for the file and click on the **Open** button.

Open dialog box

Printing a presentation

Click on the **File** menu ⟹ **Print** option. A **Print** dialog box appears with the following options.

1. *Print Range*: Here you instruct the printer which slides to print. It can be:
   a. Print All Slides
   b. Print Selection
   c. Print Current Slide
   d. Custom Range

2. *Number of copies*

3. *Preview*

These are the most common options defined to get the required settings before the final printouts are taken.

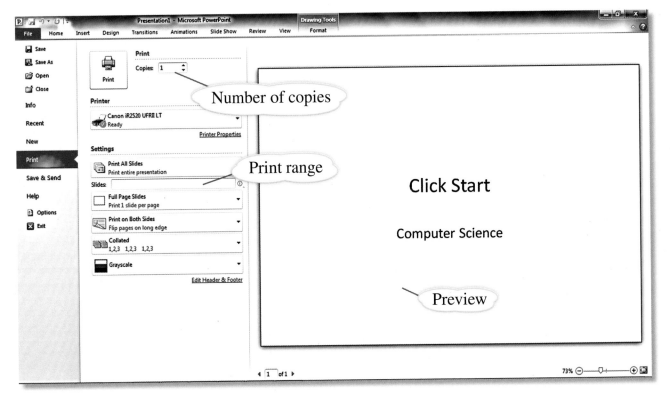

Print dialog box

Closing and exiting a presentation

To close a presentation

Click on **File** menu ⟹ **Close** option.

When you use the above option the file closes but the MS PowerPoint 2010 application continues to run.

To exit from MS PowerPoint 2010

Click on **File** menu ⟹ **Exit PowerPoint** option.

When you choose this, the MS PowerPoint 2010 application closes.

To open a presentation	**Ctrl + O**	To undo the last work	**Ctrl + Z**
To save a presentation	**Ctrl + S**	To redo or repeat	**Ctrl + Y**
To print a presentation	**Ctrl + P**	To insert a new slide	**Ctrl + M**
To close a presentation	**Ctrl + W**	To open a new presentation	**Ctrl + N**

GLOSSARY

Presentation A display about a particular topic. You can use software like MS PowerPoint to help visually display a presentation.

Slide Layout The arrangement of text and graphics on the slide.

YOU ARE HERE

8

1. Microsoft PowerPoint is the most common software program used to create presentations and slide shows.
2. A presentation consists of slides that are organised and formatted using the features of Microsoft PowerPoint.
3. The Title slide is the default slide.
4. Click on the File menu ⟹ New option to start a new presentation.
5. The Normal View displays the current slide in the Slide pane. This view is the most suited for editing the text and graphics on a slide.
6. The Slide Sorter view is useful for selecting multiple slides and changing the order of slides.
7. The Slide Show view displays the presentation as it will appear to the audience, starting with slide 1 regardless of which slide is currently displayed.
8. Click on the View tab ⟹ Slide Show option to start the slide show.
9. Click on the File menu ⟹ Open option to open an existing presentation.
10. Click on the File menu ⟹ Print option to print an existing presentation.
11. Click on the File menu ⟹ Exit PowerPoint option to quit MS PowerPoint 2010.

EXERCISE

A. True or false?

1. A MS PowerPoint presentation consists of images. ☐

2. The Slides tab displays the slides of the presentation as miniatures called thumbnails. ☐

3. The Office Theme section in the drop-down list is used to select different templates for the different slides. ☐

4. A new presentation opens with the Title Slide. ☐

5. Slide Sorter View is best for editing the text and graphics on a slide. ☐

6. To re-display the hidden pointer and/or change the pointer to a pen, press Ctrl + A. ☐

B. Match the following.

1. Ctrl + N   a. To insert a new slide

2. Ctrl + O   b. To print a presentation

3. Ctrl + P   c. To undo the last work

4. Ctrl + M   d. To open a presentation

5. Ctrl + Z   e. To create a new presentation

C. Identify the following icons and state their purpose.

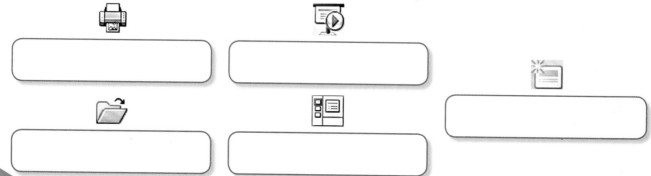

D. Answer the following questions.

1. What is a presentation?

2. What do you understand by the term Slide Layout?

3. State any five components of MS Powerpoint 2010 screen.

4. Explain the different views of a PowerPoint presentation.

5. How do you come out of a MS PowerPoint 2010 presentation without coming out of the MS PowerPoint 2010 application?

6. Name any two commonly used options present in the Print dialog box.

LAB WORK 🖥️

Complete the following activity.

1. Create a presentation on the topic 'Uses of computers' with ten slides.

2. Create the first slide as the Title Slide and include the title of the presentation and the name of the person who created it.

3. Put the text 'Thank you' on the last slide.

4. On slide numbers 2 to 9 include information about eight different uses of computers, with one on each slide with a relevant picture. For example, computers are used in hospitals to keep patient records and to diagnose them.

PROJECT WORK

Work in groups. Each group should choose a country of the world and make a presentation about it. The presentation should give important information about the country – like its capital city, language, local dance, traditional clothes, famous food, major crops, key industries etc.

- The components of the MS Powerpoint 2016 window are shown below.

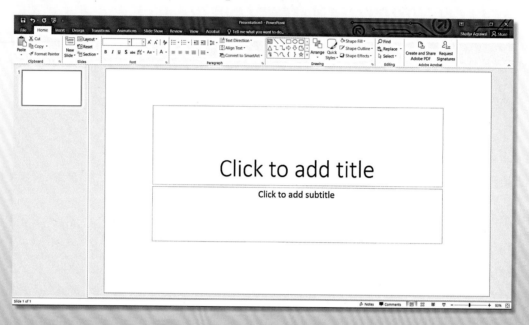

- To create a New presentation: click on the **File** menu then select
  New ⟹ Blank Presentation.

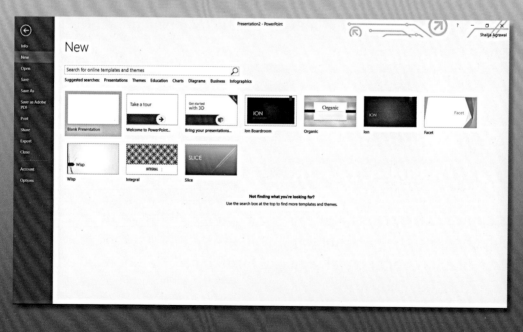

- MS PowerPoint 2016 allows you to share presentations. For this, click on **File** menu ⟹ **Share**.

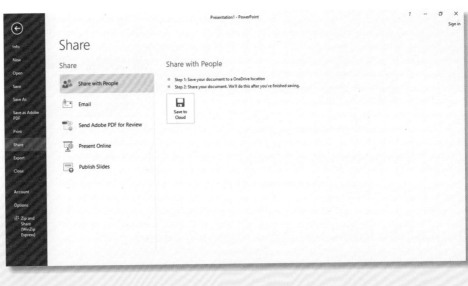

This allows you to share your presentation on your drive with other people.

The recipients can only view the presentation, or can edit it depending on the option you select at the time of sharing the file.

- In MS PowerPoint 2016, you can use **View** tab to access different views.

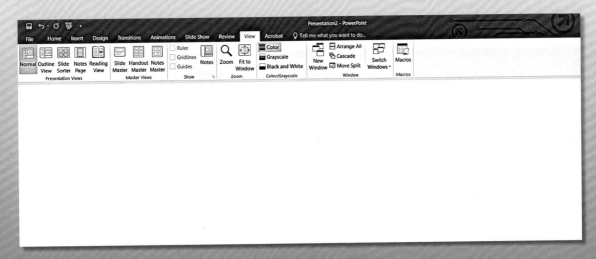

- For running a slide show, click on the **Slide Show** tab.

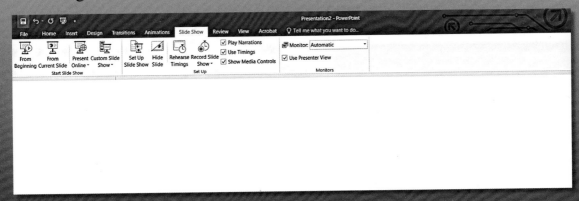

Sample Paper

Tick (✓) the correct option.

1. **Which of the following is a pointing device?**

   a. ☐   b. ☐   c. ☐   d. ☐

2. **A monitor is an output device. Which of the following is not a type of monitor?**

   a. Cathode Ray Tube (CRT) monitor ☐   c. Light Emitting Diodes (LED) monitor ☐

   b. Liquid Crystal Display (LCD) monitor ☐   d. Laser monitor ☐

3. **ALU is one of the three parts of CPU. What does ALU stand for?**

   a. Abacus Language Unit ☐   c. Arithmetic Logic Unit ☐

   b. Abstract Logic Unit ☐   d. Arithmetic Language Unit ☐

4. **Select the computer memory which is also known as volatile memory.**

   a. Read Only Memory ☐   c. Cache memory ☐

   b. Secondary memory ☐   d. Random Access Memory ☐

5. **In order to change the desktop background of the computer, right-click on the desktop and then click on the .... option.**

   a. Refresh ☐   c. Personalize ☐

   b. Gadgets ☐   d. Screen Resolution ☐

6. **Name the image that you see when the computer is left idle for some time. It disappears as soon as you click the mouse or press any key.**

   a. Screen saver ☐   b. Desktop ☐   c. Icon ☐   d. Window ☐

7. **Select the incorrect sentence from the options given below.**

   a. Every computer has a built-in calendar and clock. It keeps on working even if the computer is shut down. ☐

b. Windows Explorer works as a manager for Windows.

c. A file is a collection of related information.

d. The files are also known as directories.

8. **Which of the following option(s) is/are given in the Font group of the Home tab in MS Word 2010?**

a. Subscript

b. Strikethrough

c. Font name

d. All of the above

9. **In MS Word 2010, which of the following icons is used to change the color of the text to emphasise headings, subheadings and other text?**

a. A ▾   b. A   c. A ▾   d. ◭ ▾

10. **After selecting the text that you wish to align, click on the appropriate alignment button in the .... group of the .... tab.**

a. Styles, Home

b. Clipboard, Home

c. Paragraph, Home

d. Font, Home

11. **In Tux Paint, which tool is used for typing text on any object or stamp?**

a. Label   b. Stamp   c. Paint   d. Magic

12. **Select the correct sentence(s) with reference to Tux Paint.**

a. Open tool is present in the Picturebook.

b. It is not possible to print pictures created using Tux Paint.

c. Pictures created in Tux Paint can also be viewed as a slide show.

d. All are correct.

13. **Match the Tux Paint keyboard shortcut sequences given in Column-I with their descriptions in Column-II.**

Column-I	Column-II
a. To save a picture	i. Ctrl + O
b. To open the list of saved pictures	ii. Ctrl + S
c. To redo the last drawing action	iii. Esc key
d. To end the slide show	iv. Ctrl + R

a. a-i, b-ii, c-iv, d-iii

b. a-ii, b-i, c-iv, d-iii

c. a-ii, b-i, c-iii, d-iv

d. a-ii, b-iii, c-iv, d-i

14. Which command of MSWLogo is used to lift the pen of the turtle from the screen?

    a. PENSHIFT ☐   b. PENMOVE ☐   c. PENDOWN ☐   d. PENUP ☐

15. A .... is a memory container which holds a value.

    a. Variable ☐   b. Storage area ☐ c. Cache ☐   d. Container ☐

16. Fill in the blanks with reference to commands used in MSWLogo. The ...... command displays the turtle which was hidden by using the .... command.

    a. HT, ST ☐   b. ST, HT ☐   c. HD, SD ☐   d. SD, HD ☐

17. The SETPENSIZE command changes the size of the pen of the turtle in MSWLogo. Which of the following shows the correct version of this command?

    a. SETPENSIZE [NUM1 NUM2, NUM3], here NUM 1 is the height, NUM 2 is the width and NUM3 is the length. ☐

    b. SETPENSIZE [NUM1 NUM2], here NUM 1 is the width and NUM 2 is the height. ☐

    c. SETPENSIZE [NUM1 NUM2], here NUM 1 is the height and NUM 2 is the width. ☐

    d. SETPENSIZE [NUM1 NUM2], here NUM 1 is the length and NUM 2 is the width. ☐

18. Which of the following is true with reference to the MAKE command in MSWLogo?

    a. It is used to assign a value to a constant. ☐
    b. It is used to assign a value to a string. ☐
    c. It is used to assign a value to an operator. ☐
    d. It is used to assign a value to a variable. ☐

19. In MS PowerPoint 2010, select the shortcut to go to the next slide.

    a. Page Up ☐   b. Page Down ☐   c. Ctrl + Home ☐   d. Ctrl + End ☐

20. Which of the following is not a view in MS PowerPoint 2010?

    a. Normal view ☐   c. Slide Sorter view ☐
    b. Data view ☐   d. Slide Show ☐